Developing RESTful Web Services with Jersey 2.0

Create RESTful web services smoothly using the robust Jersey 2.0 and JAX-RS APIs

Sunil Gulabani

[PACKT] open source
PUBLISHING
community experience distilled

BIRMINGHAM - MUMBAI

Developing RESTful Web Services with Jersey 2.0

First published: November 2013

Production Reference: 2070214

Published by Packt Publishing Ltd.
Livery Place
35 Livery Street
Birmingham B3 2PB, UK

ISBN 978-1-78328-829-8

www.packtpub.com

Cover Image by Aniket Sawant (aniket_sawant_photography@hotmail.com)

Credits

Author
Sunil Gulabani

Reviewers
Ketan Parmar
Daniel Rodríguez Millán

Acquisition Editor
Rubal Kaur

Commissioning Editor
Shaon Basu

Technical Editor
Mrunmayee Patil

Copy Editors
Mradula Hegde
Dipti Kapadia
Alfida Paiva

Project Coordinator
Akash Poojary

Proofreader
Clyde Jenkins

Indexer
Monica Mehta

Graphics
Abhinash Sahu

Production Coordinator
Nilesh R. Mohite

Cover Work
Nilesh R. Mohite

About the Author

Sunil Gulabani is a software engineer based in Ahmedabad, Gujarat (India). He completed his graduation in Commerce from S M Patel Institute of Commerce (SMPIC) and Masters in Computer Applications from Ahmedabad Education Society Institute of Computer Studies (AESICS). He has been a top ranker while pursuing his master's degree. He has also presented a paper "Effective Label Matching For Automated Evaluation of Use Case Diagrams" on Technology For Education (T4E) — IIIT. Hyderabad, an IEEE Conference, along with senior lecturers, Vinay Vachharajani and Dr. Jyoti Pareek.

He has been working since 2011 as a software engineer, and is Cloud technology savvy. He has experience in developing enterprise solutions using Java (EE), Apache SOLR, RESTful web services, GWT, SmartGWT, Amazon web services (AWS), Redis, Memcache, MongoDB, and so on. He has a keen interest in system architecture and integration, data modeling, relational databases, and mapping with NoSQL for high throughput.

Apart from that, he takes interest in writing tech blogs and is actively involved in a knowledge-sharing community named Java User Group Ahmedabad (JUG-Ahmedabad).

You can visit him online at `http://www.sunilgulabani.com` and follow him on Twitter at twitter.com/sunil_gulabani, or reach him directly at `sunil_gulabani@yahoo.com`.

I would like to express my heartiest thanks to my parents and family members who supported me at each and every level of my career. I would also like to convey thanks to my friends and colleagues without whom jumping to the next step of my career would not be possible. And thanks to the Packt Publishing team, who gave me an opportunity to author this book.

About the Reviewers

Ketan Parmar (aka KPBird) has been a Java enthusiast since the last seven years. He started working in various technologies in Java, and explored all three areas (SE, ME, and EE). He is currently working as a Technical Lead.

His constant urge for finding best solutions using emerging technology made him pursue Ph.D. (Mobile Grid Computing). He has provided lots of solutions on Stack Overflow, and has contributed on various blogs and sites.

He is passionate about Java, Android, grid computing, user interface, and open source software (OSS). He is currently exploring big data. He has been an eminent speaker on Java Enterprise and Android Mobile related tools and technologies. He is the leader and founder of JUGAhmedabad (Java User Group Ahmedabad).

Daniel Rodriguez is a software architect for Java server-side development. He has background experience on high demand servers in the Electric Power Industry. He is also a software hobbyist who likes to study all frameworks available, searching for the perfect tool for the perfect job.

He has worked for 10 years on banking, public administration, and electric power industry, from logistics field work devices to mainframe servers. He is currently working as a senior software developer at Mobivery, a startup focused on client and server development for mobile projects.

He is the author of the book Java Game Programming (Programación de videojuegos en Java) focused on game architecture for mobile phones.

I would like to thank my baby girl Miriam for sleeping enough time for me to review this book.

www.PacktPub.com

Support files, eBooks, discount offers, and more

You might want to visit www.PacktPub.com for support files and downloads related to your book.

Did you know that Packt offers eBook versions of every book published, with PDF and ePub files available? You can upgrade to the eBook version at www.PacktPub.com and as a print book customer, you are entitled to a discount on the eBook copy. Get in touch with us at service@packtpub.com for more details.

At www.PacktPub.com, you can also read a collection of free technical articles, sign up for a range of free newsletters and receive exclusive discounts and offers on Packt books and eBooks.

PACKTLIB®

http://PacktLib.PacktPub.com

Do you need instant solutions to your IT questions? PacktLib is Packt's online digital book library. Here, you can access, read and search across Packt's entire library of books.

Why Subscribe?

- Fully searchable across every book published by Packt
- Copy and paste, print and bookmark content
- On demand and accessible via web browser

Free Access for Packt account holders

If you have an account with Packt at www.PacktPub.com, you can use this to access PacktLib today and view nine entirely free books. Simply use your login credentials for immediate access.

Table of Contents

Preface

This book is for developing the JAX-RS 2.0 RESTful web services using Java. It provides an understanding of new features of JAX-RS 2.0, along with practical examples for the server and client side. It also covers implementation of different media representations, such as JSON, XML, and multipart. Apart from this, we have also included the modern HTML5-feature of Server-Sent Events (SSE). SSE is basically used for real-time applications, where a server pushes events to the client. Lastly, we described how to generate an XML specification named Web Application Description Language (WADL) of the web services.

What this book covers

Chapter 1, Getting Started, gives a brief note regarding the new features that have been introduced in JAX-RS 2.0, such as client API, filters and interceptors, and client-side and server-side asynchronous. It also contains some other prominent features, such as listing of modules and dependencies that are used for implementing JAX-RS 2.0.

Chapter 2, Server API, covers how to create resource classes and methods, usage of parameter annotations to access user-defined values, and subresources to consume specific resource methods. We will see when the root-resource classes are accessible, and the rules for injecting the path annotations to access values. Lastly, we will learn how to load the resource classes using different methods of the Application model, ResourceConfig, and Without Application Model.

Chapter 3, Client API, shows how to consume the RESTful web services that are using the JAX-RS client API. We will cover how to call web services for different HTTP headers and *Param annotations, so that we can then perform all the CRUD operations using this client API. JAX-RS is a wrapper class of the HTTP, so we can use any web services that are based on the HTTP protocol. JAX-RS client API follows the uniformity that implements the REST architecture.

Chapter 4, Common Media-Type Representations, covers different representations of the data. Data representation is the primary decision for any application. We need to decide an appropriate representation on the basis of the client that will consume the web services. We will also go through the implementation of different representations on the server side as well as the client side.

Chapter 5, Server-Sent Events (SSE), covers how to create a connection between the client/server and maintain the connection at the server's end. This is needed to push the data from the server to the client without any new request initiated by the client. This type of mechanism is basically used for applications such as chatting, stock market, or any real-time data-providing applications.

Chapter 6, WADL, describes Web Application Description Language (WADL), which is a skeleton of the deployed RESTful web service.

What you need for this book

- Understanding of RESTful web services
- Java EE
- Eclipse IDE
- JAX-RS 1.0 knowledge (optional)

Who this book is for

This book is intended for the Java EE developers who are building the application on the REST architecture. This is a quick handbook for learning JAX-RS 2.0. Developers should be having knowledge about the RESTful web services and not mandated to JAX-RS 1.0.

Conventions

In this book, you will find a number of styles of text that distinguish between different kinds of information. Here are some examples of these styles, and an explanation of their meaning.

Code and the output being generated by the code are added to the book as screenshots.

A block of code is set as follows:

```
@Path("/getResource")
public class GetResource {
```

```
        @GET
        public String get() {
            return "Hello World!!!";
        }

        @GET
        @Path("{name}")
        public Response greetUser(@PathParam("name") String name){
            returnResponse.status(200).entity("Hello, " +
            name).build();
        }
    }
```

New terms and **important words** are shown in bold. Words that you see on the screen, in menus, or dialog boxes for example, appear in the text like this: "clicking the **Next** button moves you to the next screen".

[Warnings or important notes appear in a box like this.]

[Tips and tricks appear like this.]

Reader feedback

Feedback from our readers is always welcome. Let us know what you think about this book—what you liked or may have disliked. Reader feedback is important for us to develop titles that you really get the most out of.

To send us general feedback, simply send an e-mail to `feedback@packtpub.com` or `sunil_gulabani@yahoo.com`, and mention the book title via the subject of your message.

If there is a topic that you have expertise in and you are interested in either writing or contributing to a book, see our author guide on `www.packtpub.com/authors`.

Customer support

Now that you are the proud owner of a Packt book, we have a number of things to help you to get the most from your purchase.

Downloading the example code

You can download the example code files for all Packt books you have purchased from your account at `http://www.packtpub.com`. If you purchased this book elsewhere, you can visit `http://www.packtpub.com/support` and register to have the files e-mailed directly to you.

Errata

Although we have taken every care to ensure the accuracy of our content, mistakes do happen. If you find a mistake in one of our books—maybe a mistake in the text or the code—we would be grateful if you would report this to us. By doing so, you can save other readers from frustration and help us improve subsequent versions of this book. If you find any errata, please report them by visiting `http://www.packtpub.com/submit-errata`, selecting your book, clicking on the **errata submission form** link, and entering the details of your errata. Once your errata are verified, your submission will be accepted and the errata will be uploaded on our website, or added to any list of existing errata, under the Errata section of that title. Any existing errata can be viewed by selecting your title from `http://www.packtpub.com/support`.

Piracy

Piracy of copyright material on the Internet is an ongoing problem across all media. At Packt, we take the protection of our copyright and licenses very seriously. If you come across any illegal copies of our works, in any form, on the Internet, please provide us with the location address or website name immediately so that we can pursue a remedy.

Please contact us at `copyright@packtpub.com` with a link to the suspected pirated material.

We appreciate your help in protecting our authors, and our ability to bring you valuable content.

Questions

You can contact us at `questions@packtpub.com` or `sunil_gulabani@yahoo.com` if you are having a problem with any aspect of the book, and we will do our best to address it.

1
Getting Started

This chapter provides readers with a brief introduction on JAX-RS 2.0. It also includes the principles required to be followed in RESTful web services and the new features that have been introduced in JAX-RS 2.0, such as client API, filters and interceptors, client-side and server-side asynchronous. It also contains some other prominent features, such as listing of modules and dependencies that are used for implementing JAX-RS 2.0. Besides the previously mentioned features, it also provides a demonstration of JAX-RS 2.0 with examples.

What is JAX-RS 2.0?

JAX-RS 2.0 is a framework that helps you in writing the RESTful web services on the client side as well as on the server side. **Jersey 2.0** is the reference implementation of the JAX-RS 2.0 (JSR 339 specification). Along with the enhancements in Java EE 7, JAX-RS 2.0 has also been revised dramatically.

The following is a list of the RESTful principles that must be followed:

- An ID should be assigned to everything
- Things should be linked together
- A common set of methods must be used
- Multiple representations should be allowed
- Stateless communication must be kept

Before moving ahead, let's look at the existing features of JAX-RS 1.0:

- POJO-based Resource API
- Provides access to the resource classes using HTTP
- Format (content types) independence
- Container (web server) independence
- Inclusion in Java EE

Features of JAX-RS 2.0

JAX-RS 2.0 remains consistent with the central theme of Java EE 7, but it contains other long-awaited APIs too. These APIs are mostly focused around what is referred to as *Simplified API*. They can be categorized as follows:

Client API	The specifications in the earlier versions of JAX-RS were only accountable for a server-side API for the RESTful calls. However, the same resulted into the development of different implementers of the server API, that is, **Jersey** and **RESTEasy**. This led to the independent development of a client-side API. Now, JAX-RS 2.0 has a Client API that provides support to the server-side specification. This feature is a major incorporation of the previous version of the Jersey Client API. This can be summarized as: • Low-level HTTP Client APIs • Shared APIs with Server APIs • Compatible with some JAX-RS 1.0 implementations
Filters and interceptors	This JAX-RS 2.0 specification is accountable for the client and server filters. In the case of the Client API, implementers provided their own versions of these filters for the client and server. This JAX-RS 2.0 specification, however, absorbs the same into its API. Things that can be done through this specification are: • Customization of JAX-RS implementations through well-defined extension points • Logging, Compression, Security, and so on can be achieved • Shared APIs with Server APIs • Compatibility with some JAX-RS 1.0 implementations using some different semantics can be achieved

Client-side and Server-side Asynchronous	This feature allows a request to be dispatched in a nonblocking manner, while the results are made available asynchronously. Also, long-running requests on the server side that are I/O bound can be dispatched. This releases the application server thread and enables it to service other requests. It helps in accomplishing the following tasks: • Allows free running of different threads at the server side • Request threads can be suspended and resumed as per the need • Servlet 3 async support • Provides Client API support
Improved Connection Negotiation	This feature helps in automatically determining the response type even if client specification is already present.
Validation	This feature consists of: • Services-enabled data validation • Bean Validation • Inline-constraint annotations on: Fields and properties Request parameters Methods based on response entity Resource classes, that is, path validation using regular expressions
HyperMedia as the Engine of Application State (HATEOAS)	This feature is an important aspect of the RESTful architecture. HATEOAS allows us to provide hyperlinks/URIs in the request/response of the web services. This can be compared with the hyperlinks in an HTML form.

However, Jersey 2.0 can be deployed on several web containers that support Servlet 2.5 or higher, Grizzly 2 HTTP server (which is also the default server for testing), and OSGi containers. For the new async feature of JAX-RS 2.0, **Server-Side Events** (**SSE**), we need containers supporting Servlet 3.0.

Ease of using and reusing JAX-RS artifacts

As a part of Java EE 7, it is easy to create RESTful web services using JAX-RS 2.0. Using JAX-RS annotations, we can map the POJO resource class to the URIs and the URI templates. Using annotations, it becomes easier to develop web services. Different `@*Param` annotations are available to access the values of the user request:

- `@PathParam`
- `@QueryParam`
- `@MatrixParam`
- `@HeaderParam`
- `@CookieParam`
- `@FormParam`
- `@DefaultValue`
- `@Context`

JAX-RS also supports all the Java data types to be supplied in the `@*Param` annotations. There are other APIs available to create the RESTful web services, but mostly they require more coding. However, in the Jersey implementation of JAX-RS, it is simpler and easier to create the RESTful web services. JAX-RS manages to encode and decode the request/response content according to the media type it mentioned.

Modules and dependencies

To provide backward compatibility, all Jersey applications are compiled with Java SE 6. Thus, we can run our Jersey application on Java SE 6 easily though JAX-RS 2.0 is part of Java EE 7.

To create Jersey-based applications, we require several dependencies and for other modules, we require third-party dependencies. Jersey dependencies are loosely-coupled and separated according to the module dependencies. Jersey dependencies are lightweight, so our application has much complexity for dependencies and creation of the RESTful web services.

The following are the core Jersey modules:

- Jersey Core
- jersey-client
- jersey-common
- jersey-server

> You can download the Jersey Core JAX-RS 2.0 Bundle from:
>
> `http://repo1.maven.org/maven2/org/glassfish/jersey/bundles/jaxrs-ri/2.0/jaxrs-ri-2.0.zip`

Apart from these dependencies, there are Jersey Containers, Connectors, Media, Extensions, Test Framework, and Glassfish Bundles. These dependencies can be easily plugged. You can find Jersey 2.0 binaries on the Jersey 2.0 Maven repository,

`http://repo1.maven.org/maven2/org/glassfish/jersey/`,

and on

`https://maven.java.net/content/repositories/releases/org/glassfish/jersey/`.

Creating a new project

The first step for creating a new project is to accumulate the required tools:

- Java JDK (Version 6 or higher)
- Eclipse IDE (Juno)
- Apache Tomcat Server (Version 7) or Glassfish Server (Version 4.0)
- Jersey Framework

Firstly, we will create a web project using Eclipse IDE. Go to **File** | **New** | **Others** | **Dynamic Web Project**. Follow the steps, and after the project is created, add the following libraries into the classpath:

- `asm-all-repackaged-2.2.0-b14.jar`
- `cglib-2.2.0-b14.jar`
- `guava-14.0.1.jar`
- `hk2-api-2.2.0-b14.jar`
- `hk2-locator-2.2.0-b14.jar`
- `hk2-utils-2.2.0-b14.jar`
- `javax.annotation-api-1.2.jar`
- `javax.inject-2.2.0-b14.jar`
- `javax.ws.rs-api-2.0.jar`

- `jersey-client-2.2.jar`
- `jersey-common-2.2.jar`
- `jersey-container-servlet-core-2.2.jar`
- `jersey-server-2.2.jar`
- `osgi-resource-locator-1.0.1.jar`
- `validation-api-1.1.0.Final.jar`

Now, we need to configure `web.xml` to the bound Jersey Container with the resources packages:

```
...........
<servlet>
  <servlet-name>simpleJerseyExample</servlet-name>
  <servlet-
    class>org.glassfish.jersey.servlet.ServletContainer</servlet-
    class>
  <init-param>
    <param-name>jersey.config.server.provider.packages</param-
      name>
    <param-value>com.demo</param-value>
  </init-param>
  <load-on-startup>1</load-on-startup>
</servlet>

<servlet-mapping>
  <servlet-name>simpleJerseyExample</servlet-name>
  <url-pattern>/services/*</url-pattern>
</servlet-mapping>
...........
```

A servlet container is treated as a controller to redirect the specified resource that is being called. `jersey.config.server.provider.packages` maps the resources that are available in the `com.demo` package. So, whenever any resource is being requested, `ServletContainer` checks into the `com.demo` package for the resource URI and serves the request accordingly.

The next step is to create the `Resource` class that contains the business logic:

```
package com.demo;

import javax.ws.rs.Path;
import javax.ws.rs.Get;
import javax.ws.rs.core.MediaType;
import javax.ws.rs.Produces;

/**
*    helloWorld Root Resource
*/
@Path("helloWorld")
public class HelloWorldResource{

  @GET
  @PRODUCES(MediaType.TEXT_PLAIN)
  public String greet(){
    return "Hello World!!!";
  }
}
```

Downloading the example code

You can download the example code files for all Packt books you have purchased from your account at `http://www.packtpub.com`. If you purchased this book elsewhere, you can visit `http://www.packtpub.com/support` and register to have the files e-mailed directly to you.

A JAX-RS resource is an annotated POJO, which provides the so-called resource methods that are able to handle the HTTP requests for the URI paths bound to the resource. In the previous code, `"helloWorld"` is the resource URI:

```
@Path("helloWorld")
```

To run the application, create a WAR file and deploy it on the Apache Tomcat Server. Once the project is deployed on the Tomcat server, we are ready to consume the "helloWorld" web service. We can type the resource URL in the browser or we can use `curl`:

```
$curl http://localhost:8080/projectName/services/helloWorld
Hello World!!!
```

Summary

We have covered a brief introduction about the JAX-RS 2.0 and Jersey 2.0 features that have enriched the JAX-RS web services. We've analyzed a simple RESTful web service example that shows the basic implementation of the JAX-RS 2.0. In the next chapter, we will see how to use the Server API with different examples of complete sets of code to implement the Server-side web services.

2
Server API

In this chapter, we will look at the creation of the RESTful web service using JAX-RS 2.0. We will see how to create resource classes and methods, usage of parameter annotations to access user-defined values, and subresources to consume specific resource methods. We will also see when the root-resource classes are accessible, and the rules for injecting the path annotations to access values. Lastly, we will learn how to load the resource classes using different methods of the Application model, ResourceConfig, and Without Application Model.

Root-resource classes

The root-resource classes are **Plain Old Java Objects** (**POJO**), which are either annotated with `@Path` or have at least one method annotated with `@Path` or a request method designator, such as `@GET`, `@PUT`, `@POST`, or `@DELETE`. Resource methods are methods of a `resource` class that are annotated with a request-method designator.

Let's look at the JAX-RS annotations:

- **@Path("resource_path")**:

  The `@Path` annotation defines the path to the base URL or `resource_path`. The base URL is based on the application's name, the servlet, and the URL pattern from the `web.xml` configuration file.

- **@PathParam**:

  The `@PathParam` annotation is used to inject values from the URL into a method parameter. In this way, one can inject, say, the ID of a resource into the method for getting the correct object.

- **@GET**:

  The `@GET` annotation indicates that the method will answer to an HTTP GET request.

- **@PUT**:

  The `@PUT` annotation indicates that the method will answer to an HTTP PUT request.

- **@POST**:

  The `@POST` annotation indicates that the method will answer to an HTTP POST request.

- **@DELETE**:

  The `@DELETE` annotation indicates that the method will answer to an HTTP DELETE request.

- **@Produces(MediaType.TEXT_PLAIN)**:

  The `@Produces` annotation defines which MIME type is delivered by a method annotated with any HTTP annotated methods. In the given example, a text (`text/plain`) is produced. Other examples would be `application/xml` or `application/json`.

- **@Consumes(type)**:

  The `@Consumes` annotation defines which MIME type is consumed by this method.

@Path

The `@Path` annotation's value is a relative URI path. This is a very simple use of the `@Path` annotation. The following code example provides a simple example of a root-resource class using the JAX-RS annotations:

```
@Path("helloWorld")
public class HelloWorldResource {

    @GET
    @Produces("text/plain")
    public String sayHello() {
        return "Hello World!";
    }
}
```

In the preceding example, the Java class will be hosted at the URI path `/helloworld`. What makes JAX-RS so useful is that one can embed variables in the URIs.

URI path templates are URIs with variables that are embedded within the URI syntax. These variables are substituted during runtime so that a resource can respond to a request, based on the substituted URI. The variables are denoted by curly braces shown as follows:

- Class-level:

```
@Path("/helloWorld/{name}")
public class HelloWorldResource {

    @GET
    @Produces("text/plain")
    public String sayHello(@PathParam("name") String name) {
        return "Hello, " + name;
    }
}
```

- Method-level:

```
@Path("/helloWorld")
public class HelloWorldResource {

    @GET
    @Produces("text/plain")
    @Path("{name}")
    public String sayHello(@PathParam("name") String name) {
        return "Hello, " + name;
    }
}
```

We can also use the following code:

`@PathParam(value = "name")` instead of `@PathParam("name")`

In the previously mentioned example, a user is prompted to enter his/her name. After that, a Jersey web service, which has been configured to respond to requests to this URI path template, will respond.

For example, if the user has entered his name as "John", the web service will respond to the following URL:

```
http://localhost:8080/JAXRSDemo/services/helloWorld/John

Output:
Hello, John
```

`@PathParam` may be used on the method parameter of a request method to get the value of the name variable.

@Path with a regular expression

`@Path` also supports a complex URI matched with a regular expression via the following expression:

```
{"variable-name":"[regular-expression]"}
```

```
@Path("/helloWorld")
public class HelloWorldResource {

    @GET
    @Produces("text/plain")
    @Path("{name: ([a-zA-Z])*}")
    public String sayHello(@PathParam("name") String name) {
        return "Hello, " + name;
    }
}
```

In this given example, a user will be prompted for *only* a string literal. For example, if the user has entered his name as "John", the web service will respond to the following URL considering the following two cases, correct or wrong:

- **Correct**:

  ```
  http://localhost:8080/JAXRSDemo/services/helloWorld/John

  Output:
  Hello, John
  ```

- **Wrong**:

  ```
  http://localhost:8080/JAXRSDemo/services/helloWorld/John1987

  Output:
  HTTP Status 404, Not Found
  ```

HTTP methods

`@GET`, `@PUT`, `@POST`, and `@DELETE` are the resource method designator annotations that are defined by JAX-RS and correspond to the similarly named HTTP methods. The behavior of a resource is determined by the type of HTTP methods to which the resource is responding.

@GET

This method is used to retrieve (or read) a representation of a resource. According to the design of the HTTP specification, GET (along with HEAD) requests are used only to read data, and not to change it. They are considered to be safe when they are used in this manner. This means that they can be called without the risk of data modification or corruption. The following example shows the use of the `GET` method:

```
...
@GET
public String getUser() {
  System.out.println("GET");
  return "Hello User";
}
...
```

Here, we have used a simple method, `getUser()`. The `@GET` annotation is a request method designator defined by JAX-RS. In this example, the annotated Java method will process the HTTP GET requests. The behavior of a resource is determined by the HTTP method to which the resource would respond.

@PUT

This one is mostly used for update capabilities. We can use `@PUT` in a known resource URI with the request body containing the newly-updated representation of the original resource.

However, it can also be used to create a resource in the case where the resource ID is chosen by the client instead of the server. The following example shows the use of this method:

```
@PUT
public void updateUser(String userData) {
    System.out.println("PUT");
    System.out.println("User Data: " + userData);
}
```

In the previous example, the `PUT` request has a payload associated with it that is stored in the `userData` variable.

@POST

`POST` is usually used for creation of new resources. The following example shows the use of the `POST` method, where the person can access the values using the `FormParam` annotation:

```
@POST
public void addUser(@FormParam("id") String id,@FormParam("name")
String name){
     System.out.println("POST");
     System.out.println("Id: " + id);
     System.out.println("Name: " + name);
}
```

Or we can also use the POST method to access the values using the `MultivaluedMap` annotation:

```
@POST
public String addUser(MultivaluedMap<String, String> formData) {
     System.out.println("Form Data: " + formData);
     return "User added successfully.";
}
```

In the previous example, one can access the ID and name parameters that are embedded in a form.

@DELETE

The use of `DELETE` is easy to understand. It is used to delete a resource identified by a URI:

```
@DELETE
@Path("{name}")
public void delete(@PathParam("name")String name) {
  System.out.println("DELETE: " + name);
}
```

@Produces

This annotation specifies the type of output a method (or web service) will produce. `@Produces` are defined at the following two levels:

- Class-level:

  In this level, all the methods in a resource can produce the specified MIME types by default.

- Method-level:

  This level overrides the specified MIME types at the class level.

If none of the methods in a resource are able to produce the MIME type in a client request, the JAX-RS runtime sends back an HTTP **406 Not Acceptable** error. If the annotation is not present at any level, by default the "text/html" media type is returned.

`@Produces` can accept multiple MIME types also:

```
@Path("/helloWorld")
@Produces("text/plain")
public class HelloWorldResource {
    @GET
    public String greet() {
        ...
    }

    @GET
    @Produces("text/html")
    public String greetUser() {
        ...
    }
}
```

In the previous example, the `greet()` method will produce the "text/plain" MIME type, which is of a class-level MIME type, whereas the `greetUser()` method will override the class-level MIME type, "text/plain", to specify the MIME type as "text/html".

It is also possible to provide multiple MIME types, as shown in the following example:

```
@GET
@Produces({"application/xml", "application/json"})
public String greet() {
    ...
}
```

In the previous example, this method will be served for any specified MIME type. Thus, it becomes easier to invoke where multiple client requests with different MIME types.

@Consumes

The `@Consumes` annotation is used to specify the MIME types that a method (or web service) can consume. `@Consumes` is defined at the following two levels:

- Class-level:

  All the methods in a resource can produce the specified MIME types by default.

- Method-level:

  It overrides the specified MIME types at the class level.

If a resource is unable to consume the MIME type of a client request, the JAX-RS runtime sends back an HTTP 415 (**Unsupported Media Type**) error. If the annotation is not present at any level, then by default, the "text/html" media type is returned.

`@Consumes` can also accept multiple MIME types, for example:

```
@Path("/helloWorld")
@Consumes("multipart/related")
public class HelloWorldResource {
    @POST
    public String processMultipart(MimeMultipart multipartData) {
        ...
    }

    @POST
    @Consumes("application/x-www-form-urlencoded")
    public String processForm(FormURLEncodedProperties formData) {
        ...
    }
}
```

In this example, the `processMultipart()` method will accept a class-level MIME type, "multipart/related", whereas `processForm` will override the class-level MIME type, and it will serve as a specified MIME type, `application/x-www-form-urlencoded`.

Parameter annotations

Parameter's annotations are used to retrieve values from the request. The different types of parameter annotations are listed as follows:

- `@PathParam`
- `@QueryParam`
- `@MatrixParam`
- `@HeaderParam`
- `@CookieParam`

- `@FormParam`
- `@BeanParam`

@PathParam

`@PathParam` is a parameter annotation that enables you to map a variable URI path's fragments into your method call. The following example shows the use of the `@PathParam` method:

```
@Path("/userService")
public class UserResource {
    ...
    @GET
    @Path("{name}")
    public String getUserByName(@PathParam("name")String name) {
        return name;
    }
    ...
}
```

In the example, the `getUserByName()` method takes a parameter as a name. We can access the URI parameter using `PathParam`. It binds the URI template's parameter to the parameter that is defined in the `getUserByName()` method.

@QueryParam

This annotation allows you to map a URI query string parameter or a URL form encoded parameter to your method invocation. The following example shows the use of the `@QueryParam` method:

```
@Path("/userService")
public class UserResource {
    ...
    @GET
    @Path("/queryParam")
    public String getUser(@QueryParam("name")String name) {
        System.out.println("Name: " + name);
        return name;
    }
    ...
}
```

In the previous example, the getUser() method and the QueryParam annotation take care of mapping a query parameter (name) in a request to a method parameter respectively.

```
URI Pattern: /services/userService/queryParam?name=John
```

In URI Pattern, /userService is the root-resource path and /queryParam is the resource method path, using which getUser(String) will be invoked. We embedded the name parameter in URI as query string and John as value.

@DefaultValue

At times, we have to keep optional parameters in request, so that we can assign a default value using `@DefaultValue`. The `DefaultValue` annotation can be used with the following annotations:

- `@PathParam`
- `@QueryParam`
- `@MatrixParam`
- `@FormParam`
- `@HeaderParam`
- `@CookieParam`

Let's look at the example of `@DefaultValue`:

```
@GET
@Path("/queryParam")
public String getUser(
    @QueryParam("name")String name,
    @DefaultValue("15") @QueryParam("age") String age) {
    System.out.println("Name: " + name);
    System.out.println("Age: " + age);
    return name;
}
```

Here, you can see that the age parameter has been assigned DefaultValue:

```
URI Pattern: /services/userService/queryParam?name=John
URI Pattern: /services/userService/queryParam?name=John&age=20
```

Both the URI patterns are correct. In the first URI, we haven't mentioned "age" parameter as query string, so application detects automatically and invoke matching resource method. And application appends the missing "age" parameter with the default value as "15". In the first URI, the response will be:

```
Name: John
Age: 15
```

For the second URI, the response will be:

```
Name: John
Age: 20
```

So, whenever there is any optional parameter for caution of error prone, you can set the default value.

@MatrixParam

Matrix parameters are a set of `name=value` pairs embedded in the URI path, for example:

```
URI Pattern: /service/getUserById/1;name=John;age=10
```

In the preceding URI, the matrix parameters are `name=John` and `age=10`, separated by a semi colon (`;`). It represents resources that are noted by their attributes as well as their IDs.

```
@GET
@Path("/getUserById/{userId}")
public Response getUserById(
    @PathParam("userId") String userId,
    @MatrixParam("name") String name,
    @DefaultValue("15") @MatrixParam("age") String age) {

        return Response
        .status(200)
        .entity("Id: " + userId + ", Name: " + name + ", Age: " + age)
        .build();
    }
```

In the example, the `getUserById()` method takes three parameters, `userId` as the path parameter, which is mandatory, and `name` and `age` as the matrix parameters. If you don't provide values in the URL path, then the value set by default is null.

@HeaderParam

The `@HeaderParam` annotation maps a request HTTP header to your method parameters, for example:

```
@GET
@Path("/getUserAgent")
public String getUserDevice(@HeaderParam("user-agent") String
userAgent,
@HeaderParam("Content-Type") MediaType contentType) {

    rcturn "User Agent: " + userAgent + ", Content-Type: " +
      contentType ;
}
```

In the previous example, the getUserDevice() method provides us with the header information of the request. At times, we need to provide a response on the basis of the request header that might be browser-specific, mobile-specific, or content type-specific.

```
URI Pattern: /services/userService/getUserAgent
```

```
$ curl -X GET -H "Content-Type:application/json"
  http://localhost:8080/Chapter2/services/userService/getUserAgent
```

In the URI, "/userService" is the root-resource path and "/getUserAgent" is the resource method that will invoke the getUserDevice() method. We embedded the header value for Content-Type so that appropriate resource method to be invoked. getUserDevice(userAgent, contentType) will be invoked and application dynamically embeds the header values for userAgent and contentType from the incoming request.

@CookieParam

Cookies are special types of HTTP headers. They are made up of name or value pairs that are passed to the resource implementation. The cookie is passed to-and-fro between the provider and the consumer with each request/response. Only consumers can modify the cookies. They are used to maintain sessions and store settings and other data.

The `@CookieParam` annotation allows you to inject the value of a cookie or an object representation of an HTTP request cookie into your method invocation:

```
@GET
@Path("/getCookies")
public String getCookies(@CookieParam("sessionid") int sessionId) {
  return "Session Id: " + sessionId;
}
```

In the example, the `getCookies()` method provides the value of the `sessionId` stored in the cookie. We can retrieve any value stored in the cookie using the `CookieParam` annotation. A default value can also be specified using the `@ DefaultValue` annotation as shown:

```
@GET
@Path("/getCookies")
public String getCookies(
    @DefaultValue("10") @CookieParam("sessionid") int sessionId) {
      return "Session Id: " + sessionId;
}
```

Sometimes, we need more information than the value itself. For that, we can use the `Cookie` class instead of the primitive datatype, for example:

```
@GET
@Path("/getCookies")
public String getCookies(@CookieParam("user-agent") Cookie
  userAgentCookie) {
    return
    "Name: " + userAgentCookie.getName() +
    "Value: " + userAgentCookie.getValue() +
    "Domain: " + userAgentCookie.getDomain() +
    "Path: " + userAgentCookie.getPath() +
    "Version: " + userAgentCookie.getVersion();
}
```

The table describing the methods of the Cookie object is as follows:

Method	Description
`getName()`	Corresponds to the string name of the cookie
`getValue()`	Corresponds to the string value of the cookie
`getDomain()`	Specifies the DNS name
`getPath()`	Corresponds to the URI path from where the request is being called
`getVersion()`	Defines the format of the cookie header

@FormParam

The `@FormParam` annotation can be used when a request body is of the media type, `application/x-www-form-urlencoded`. We can inject single parameters into the resource method invocation. Let's look at the following example:

```
@POST
@Path("/addUser")
public void addUser(
    @FormParam("name") String name,
    @FormParam("id") String id){
        System.out.println("Add User:");
        System.out.println("Id: " + id);
        System.out.println("Name: " + name);
    }
```

In the preceding example, `name` and `id` are form parameters that are being injected into the `addUser()` resource method:

```
$ curl -X POST -d "name=John&id=100" http://localhost:8080/Chapter2/
services/userService/addUser
```

Here `/userService` is the root-resource path and `/addUser` is the resource method. In the curl request we embedded the form data for `name` and `id` as `John` and `100` respectively. We can also use `MultivaluedMap<String,String>` to get all values of the HTML form, shown as follows:

```
@POST
@Path("/addUser")
public String addUser(MultivaluedMap<String, String> formData) {
    return "Form Data: " + formData;
}
```

It is not mandatory for the form's data to be encoded. Mostly, MultivaluesMap's data are automatically decoded by the JAX-RS implementations.

@BeanParam

This annotation allows injection of the parameters into a single bean. A bean annotated with `@BeanParam` containing any properties and other parameter annotations (such as `@PathParam`, `@QueryParam`, `@MatrixParam`, `@HeaderParam`, `@CookieParam`, `@FormParam`) will be mapped with request values.

Therefore, instead of providing request values, such as parameter annotations (for example, `@PathParam`, `@QueryParam`, `@MatrixParam`, `@HeaderParam`, `@CookieParam`, and `@FormParam`) into a method parameter, the `@BeanParam` annotation can be used. The `@BeanParam` annotation is used for aggregation of more request parameters into a single bean. Let's take a look at the following example:

```
public class UserBean {

    @PathParam("id")
    private String id;

    @MatrixParam("name")
    private String name;

    @MatrixParam("age")
    private String age;

    @DefaultValue("No address provided")
    @QueryParam("address")
    private String address;

    @HeaderParam("user-agent")
    private String userAgent;

    public String toString(){
        return
```

```
            "Id: " + id +
            "\nName: " + name +
            "\nAge: " + age +
            "\nAddress: " + address +
            "\nUser Agent: " + userAgent + "\n" ;
        }
    }
```

This is the UserBean that we will inject into the resource method:

```
@Path("/beanResource")
public class BeanResource {

    @GET
    @Path("/getUserDetails/{id}")
    public String getUser(@BeanParam UserBean userBean) {
        return "User Bean: " + userBean.toString();
    }
}
```

In this example, the `UserBean` fields are being mapped with their respective parameter annotations. You can run the example from a browser using the following URI:

```
URI Pattern:

$ curl -X GET http://exampe.com/services/beanResource/getUserDetails/1
;name=John;age=25?address=USA
```

Subresources

The `@Path` annotation is used for the identification of the resource that is to be called for the specific request. It can be defined at the following two levels:

- Class-level
- API-level

Class-level `@Path` annotations are termed as the root-resource classes, and the methods are defined as resource methods, whereas API-level `@Path` annotations point directly to specific methods under the root-resource classes, which are defined as subresource methods. The following example shows the use of the subresources:

```
@Path("/userService")
public class UserResource {

    @GET
```

```
    public String getUser() {
        return "John";
    }

    @GET
    @Path("/getUserName")
    public String getUserName() {
        return "John";
    }
}
```

In this example, `getUserName()` is the subresource method, as we have explicitly defined the path of the method. We can also assign regular expressions in the URI template for the root-resource class and the subresource methods. When the request URI is userService, the first resource method, getUser(), will be invoked, and when the request URI is "userService/getUserName", the second method, getUserName(), will be invoked:

```
URI Pattern: http://localhost:8080/Chapter2/services/userService/
getUserName
```

In the URI, `/userService` is the root-resource path and `/getUserName` is the resource method that will invoke the `getUserName()` method in which we explicitly defined the path /getUserName.

We can also create subresource locators where methods under the root-resource classes are not annotated by any HTTP headers. In fact, these HTTP header resource methods will be created in different resource classes where we redirect the request from the root-resource method class. This helps in easier management of the code, and each subresource will be loosely coupled. Let's look at the example:

```
@Path("/userService")
public class UserResource {
                ......... .
    @Path("/getAddress")
    public AddressResource getAddress() {
        return new AddressResource();
    }
}

public class AddressResource {
    @GET
    public Response getUserName() {
        return Response
               .status(200)
```

```
                .entity("Address")
                .build();
        }
}
```

```
URI Pattern: http://localhost:8080/Chapter2/services/userService/
getAddress
```

In the `UserResource` class, we have a subresource method, `getAddress()`, which redirects the request to the AddressResource. This is termed as a subresource locator. Now, AddressResource is responsible for delivering the response to the request. It locates the appropriate subresource method and the method that is being invoked to serve the request.

Scope of the root-resource classes

By default, every time a new request is made, a new instance of the root-resource class is being created. The scope of the root-resource class, which is created at the time of request, is limited to that request only. This makes it easier to manage and work in isolation. It helps us in handling multiple concurrent requests to the root-resource class. We don't need to manage anything to handle multiple concurrent requests.

If we manage a single root-resource class instance to process multiple concurrent requests, we will face performance issues for the same. A new instance for every request makes it easier for JVM to go for garbage collection of the created and destroyed instance that served the request. We can also define a root-resource class as Singleton for a single instance of multiple requests.

Let's now look at the resource scopes:

- Request scope:

  By using the `@RequestScope` annotation or none, we can have a life-cycle till the request lasts. This is the default scope of the root-resource classes. For each new request, a new root-resource instance is being created and served accordingly for the first time. However, when the same root-resource method is being called, then the old instance will be used to serve the request.

- Per-lookup scope:

  The `@PerLookup` annotation creates root-resource instances for every request.

- Singleton:

  The `@Singleton` annotation allows us to create only a single instance throughout the application.

Rules of injection

Injection can be applied on fields, constructor parameters, resources, subresources, subresource locators, method parameters, and setter methods. It helps to identify which path or parameter of the request needs to be handled. Let's look at the following examples:

- Root-resource:

```
@Path("/userService")
public class UserResource {
    ...
}
```

- Fields:

```
@Path("/userService")
public class UserResource {
    ...
    @QueryParam("name")
    private String name;
    ...
}
```

- Constructor parameter:

```
@Path("/userService")
public class UserResource {

    public UserResource(@PathParam("id") int id){
        ...
    }

    @GET
    @Path("{id}")
    public String getUser() {
        ...
    }
}
```

- Resource method:

```
@Path("/userService")
public class UserResource {
    @GET
    public String getUser(@QueryParam("name")String name) {
        ...
    }
}
```

- Subresource method:

```
@Path("/userService")
public class UserResource {
    @GET
    @Path("/getUser/{name}")
    public String getUser(@PathParam("name")String name) {
        ...
    }
}
```

- Subresource locator method:

```
@Path("/userService")
public class UserResource {
    @Path("/getAddress")
    public AddressResource getAddress(@QueryParam("id")
      int id) {
        ...
    }
}
```

- Bean setter method:

```
@Path("/userService")
public class UserResource {
    @GET
    @Path("{id}")
    public String getUser() {
        ...
    }

    @PathParam("id")
    public void setId( int id){
        ...
    }
}
```

Deploying a RESTful web service

There are several ways to deploy the JAX-RS applications. Some of them are illustrated as follows:

- **Using the abstract Application class**:

  In this type, we provide all the root-resource classes to the `Application` class. So, when the server is started, we need to load the Application subclass that has injected the root-resource class. Basically, when we need to set some configuration before loading the root-resource class, we can use the Application Model. Let's look at the following example:

```
public class MainApplication extends Application {
    @Override
    public Set<Class<?>> getClasses() {
        Set<Class<?>> s = new HashSet<Class<?>>();
        s.add(HelloWorld.class);
        …. .
        return s;
    }
}
```

  In `web.xml`, the path of the Application subclass needs to be defined, as shown in the following code:

```
    ….
    <servlet>
        <servlet-name>Jersey Web Application</servlet-name>
        <servlet-class>org.glassfish.jersey.servlet.
ServletContainer</servlet-class>
        <init-param>
<param-name>javax.ws.rs.Application</param-name>
            <param-value>com.example.MainApplication</param-value>
        </init-param>
        <load-on-startup>1</load-on-startup>
    </servlet>

    <servlet-mapping>
        <servlet-name>Jersey Web Application</servlet-name>
        <url-pattern>/services/*</url-pattern>
    </servlet-mapping>
    …….
```

- **Using the ResourceConfig class**:

  The `ResourceConfig` class is used to configure a web application. Let's look at the following example:

```
public class MainApplication extends ResourceConfig{
    public MainApplication() {
        packages("com.example");
    }
}
```

  In `web.xml`, we need to define the path of the `Application` subclass:

```
    ....
    <servlet>
        <servlet-name>Jersey Web Application</servlet-name>
        <servlet-class>org.glassfish.jersey.servlet.
ServletContainer</servlet-class>
        <init-param>
<param-name>javax.ws.rs.Application</param-name>
            <param-value>com.example.MainApplication</param-value>
        </init-param>
        <load-on-startup>1</load-on-startup>
    </servlet>

    <servlet-mapping>
        <servlet-name>Jersey Web Application</servlet-name>
        <url-pattern>/services/*</url-pattern>
    </servlet-mapping>
    .......
```

  In the `MainApplication` class, we have defined the package name where all the root-resource classes exist. Now, the `ResourceConfig` class manages to load the root-resource class from a package when the server starts. We can also define multiple packages in which the root-resources classes exist, for example:

```
packages("com.example;com.example2;com.example3");
```

- **Without Application class**:

  This type of deployment process is used when we don't need to set any pre-configuration for our web application before loading the root-resource classes.

```
    .......
    <servlet>
        <servlet-name>Jersey Web Application</servlet-name>
        <servlet-class>org.glassfish.jersey.servlet.
  ServletContainer</servlet-class>
```

```
    <init-param>
        <param-name>jersey.config.server.provider.packages
</param-name>
            <param-value>com.example</param-value>
    </init-param>
    <load-on-startup>1</load-on-startup>
</servlet>

<servlet-mapping>
<servlet-name>Jersey Web Application</servlet-name>
    <url-pattern>/services/*</url-pattern>
</servlet-mapping>
```

Here, we have defined the package path where the root-resource class exists. We can also supply multiple packages for different root-resources classes, such as:

```
<param-value>com.example;com.example2;com.example3</param-value>
```

Summary

In this chapter, we covered how to create the JAX-RS web service using Jersey implementation. We also saw different aspects of the defining resource classes and their methods, how HTTP headers will be defined, and what will be the scope of the path parameter annotations. We also discussed the rules to inject path parameters into resource methods. Finally, we saw various methods to deploy our resource classes. In the next chapter, we will see how to consume these server-side web services with different HTTP annotated methods and *Param annotations.

3
Client API

In the previous chapter, we have seen how to create RESTful web services using the Jersey implementation of JAX-RS 2.0. In this chapter, we will see how to consume the RESTful web services that are using the JAX-RS client API. We will also cover how to call web services for different HTTP headers and *Param annotations, so that we can then perform all the CRUD operations using this client API. JAX-RS is a wrapper class over the HTTP, so we can use any web services that are based on the HTTP protocol. JAX-RS client API follows the uniformity that implements the REST architecture.

Consuming web services using a client

The JAX-RS client API is built on top of the HTTP protocol. It consumes all web services that are built on the HTTP protocol. Apart from this client API, there are other APIs, such as HTTPURLConnection and Apache HTTP Library, to consume web services. However, this API is harder to code and time-consuming for complex web services. So, the JAX-RS client API is wrapped in such a way that developers can find it easy to code and reuse wrapper classes as much as they can.

In the *Web Service Flow* figure, **Client** is the base to initiate the connection. We can get the client instance using the entry point, that is, the `ClientBuider` method. ClientBuilder provides a new instance every time. So, if necessary, we can create different instances for different URIs.

> Note that creating multiple client instances can be expensive.

Once we obtain the client instance, optionally, we can set properties or register filters. Filters can help in manipulating custom objects over the client and server side. Now, we create an instance of WebTarget using the `client.target()` method. We can provide either the context URI or a root-resource URI. Setting target to the context URI will allow the same target instance to call multiple individual resource URIs, and in case of setting a target to individual URIs, we can use the same target instance URI or its subresources. Setting the target to context URIs is preferable, because we need to call the same resources of single context URI. Under the `WebTarget` instance, we have a `path()` method that allows us to provide the resource URI or subresource URI.

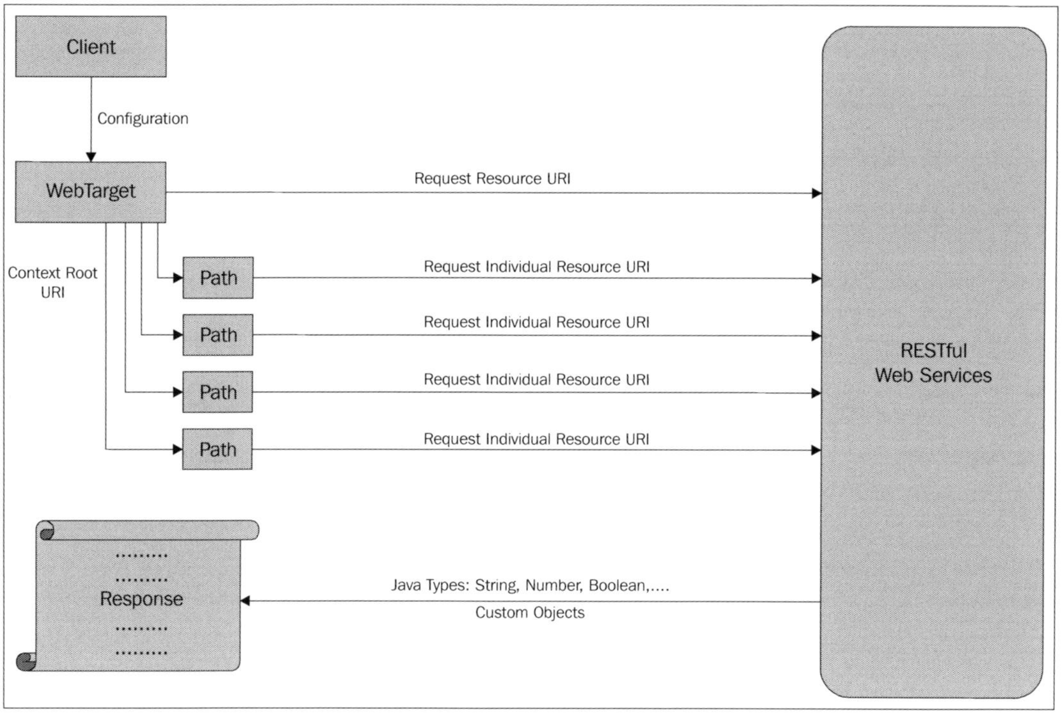

Web Service Flow

Let's look at the following example:

```
Client client = ClientBuilder.newClient();

WebTarget target = client.target("http://localhost:8080/Chapter2/
services");

target = target.path("getResource");
```

Here, we first created an instance of client using the static method of ClientBuilder. Then, from the client instance, we mapped the context root URI. For consuming specific `getResource` web service, we set the target using the `path()` method. So now, our web target points to the following location:

```
http://localhost:8080/Chapter2/services/getResource
```

We are simply calling a `getResource` method. In either way, we can receive the response from web service in "Response" or "String":

```
Response response = target.request().get();

String responseData = response.readEntity(String.class);
```

Or

```
String responseData = target.request().get(String.class);
```

By using "Response", we can know the status or access the header properties, metadata, media type, cookies, and so on, of the response received. Let's see how to consume the RESTful web service using different representation types and resource methods.

The get method

The HTTP get method invokes the request. This method is by default requested synchronously:

```
WebTarget target = client.target("http://localhost:8080/Chapter2/
services/getResource");

String responseData = target.request().get(String.class);
```

Here, we specified that the accept type will be a Java primitive type string. For consuming the get method, we have the `get(...)` method of the `Builder` class.

On the server side, it will first identify the root-resource `getResource` and then check for the matching resource method to process the request. The resource method is mapped according to the matching URI template, that is, either a subresource or the validator, or the `@Produces` media type or `@Consumes` media type is applied on the resource method.

```
@GET
public String get() {
    return "Hello World!!!";
}
```

The post method

The HTTP post method invokes the request. This method is by default requested synchronously as follows:

```
WebTarget target = client.target("http://localhost:8080/Chapter2/
services/postResource");

MultivaluedMap<String, String> postForm = new
MultivaluedHashMap<String, String>();

postForm.add("name", "John");

String responseData = target
                     .request()
                     .post(Entity.form(postForm),String.class);
```

Here, we provided `MultivaluedMap<String,String>` to pass the form parameters. It is the same as passing input types in an HTML form. `Entity.form(postForm)` creates the `application/x-www-form-urlencoded` form entity. So, we don't need to define the content type explicitly. This makes it easier for a developer to code and manage the API. For consuming the post method, we have the `post(...)` method of the `Builder` class.

On the server side, it will first identify the root-resource `getResource` and then check for the matching resource method `post(...)` to process the request. The resource method is mapped according to the matching URI template, that is, either a subresource or the validators, or the `@Produces` media type or the `@Consumes` media type is applied on the resource method:

```
@POST
public Response postForm(@FormParam("name") String name){
    return Response
           .status(200)
           .entity("Hello, "+ name)
           .build();
}
```

The put method

The HTTP put method invokes the request. This method is requested synchronously by default:

```
WebTarget target = client.target("http://localhost:8080/Chapter2/
services/putResource");

MultivaluedMap<String, String> putForm = new
MultivaluedHashMap<String, String>();
```

```
putForm.add("name", "John");

String responseData = target.request().put(Entity.
form(putForm),String.class);
```

It is the same as the post method. In order to consume the put method, we have the `put(...)` method of the `Builder` class.

On the server side, it will first identify the root-resource `getResource` and then check for the matching resource method `put()` to process the request. The resource method is mapped according to the matching URI template, that is, either a subresource or the validator, or the `@Produces` media type or the `@Consumes` media type is applied on resource method:

```
@PUT
public String put(@FormParam("name") String name){
    return "Hello, " + name;
}
```

The delete method

The HTTP delete method invokes the request. This method is requested synchronously by default as follows:

```
WebTarget target =
    client
    .target(
  "http://localhost:8080/Chapter2/services/deleteResource?name=John%20
Doe");

String responseData = target.request().delete(String.class);
```

Here, the values are passed using the Query parameter. We can also use the path parameter to pass values to the server. For consuming the delete method, we have the `delete(...)` method of the `Builder` class.

On the server side, it will first identify the root-resource `getResource` and then check for the matching resource method `delete()` to process the request. The resource method is mapped according to the matching URI template, that is, either a subresource or the validator, or the `@Produces` media type or the `@Consumes` media type that are applied on the resource method.

```
@DELETE
public String delete( @QueryParam("name") String name){
    return "Delete " + name;
}
```

The path parameter

To set the path parameters, we have a `path(String)` and `resolveTemplate (String,Object)` method to add multiple path parameters as the key/value pair. This eliminates the necessity to specify path parameters into URI. It is easier for developers to read the code and assign multiple path parameters:

```
WebTarget target = client.target("http://localhost:8080/Chapter2/
services/getResource");

String responseData =
                        target
                                .path("{id}")
                                .resolveTemplate("id", "100")
                                .request()
                                .get(String.class);
```

Here, we consumed the get method by using the path parameter. At the time of request invocation, the builder forms the URI as follows:

`http://localhost:8080/Chapter2/services/getResource/100`

On the server side, using the `@Path` and `@PathParam` annotations provided by the JAX-RS API, path parameters are mapped to the method parameter:

```
@GET
@Path("{id}")
public Response get(@PathParam("id") int id) {
    return Response.status(200).entity("Id: " + id).build();
}
```

In this example, we have used the `@PathParameter` annotation to map the `id` parameter with the request path parameter.

The query parameter

To set the query parameters, we have a `queryParam(String,Object)` method to add multiple query parameters as the key/value pair. This eliminates the need to specify query parameters into URI as follows:

```
WebTarget target = client.target( "http://localhost:8080/Chapter2/
services/getResource");

String responseData =
                        target
                                .path("subResource")
```

```
                              .queryParam("id", 1)
                              .queryParam("name", "John")
                              .request().get(String.class);
```

At the time of request invocation, the builder forms the URI as:

```
http://localhost:8080/Chapter2/services/getResource/
subResource?id=1&name=John
```

On the server side, using an `@QueryParam` annotation provided by the JAX-RS API, query parameters are mapped to the method parameter as follows:

```
@GET
@Path("/subResource")
public Response usingQueryParam(
         @DefaultValue("0") @QueryParam("id") String id,
         @DefaultValue("No Name") @QueryParam("name") String name) {
    return Response
            .status(200)
            .entity("Id: " + id + ", Name: " + name).build();
}
```

In this example, we have used the `@QueryParameter` annotation to map the `id` and `name` parameters with the request `id` and `name` parameters respectively.

The cookie parameter

To set the cookie parameters, we have a `cookie(Cookie)` method to add multiple cookies. Cookies are reliable mechanisms to remember information or maintain users' activities.

```
WebTarget target = client
.target("http://localhost:8080/Chapter2/services/getResource/
getSessionId");

Cookie cookie = new Cookie("sessionid", "100");

String responseData = target.request().cookie(cookie).get(String.
class);
```

On the server side, using an `@CookieParam` annotation provided by the JAX-RS API, cookie parameters are been mapped to the method parameters.

```
@GET
@Path("/getSessionId")
public String getSessionId(@CookieParam("sessionid") int sessionId) {
    return "Session Id: " + sessionId ;
}
```

In this example, we have used the `@CookieParameter` annotation to map the `sessionid` parameter with the request `sessionId` parameter.

The matrix parameter

To set the matrix parameters, we have the `matrixParam(String,Object)` method to add multiple matrix parameters. Matrix parameter values are converted into string objects using the `toString()` method. They are appended at the end of the URI path segments as follows:

```
WebTarget target = client.target("http://localhost:8080/Chapter2/
services/getResource");

String responseData =
                    target
                          .path("usingMatrixParam")
                          .matrixParam("id", 1)
                          .matrixParam("name", "John")
                           .request().get(String.class);
```

At the time of request invocation, the builder forms the URI as follows:

`http://localhost:8080/Chapter2/services/getResource/usingMatrixParam;id=1;name=John`

On the server side, using an `@MatrixParam` annotation provided by the JAX-RS API, matrix parameters are mapped to the method parameters:

```
@GET
@Path("usingMatrixParam")
public Response usingMatrixParam(
                  @DefaultValue("0") @MatrixParam("id") String id,
                  @DefaultValue("No Name") @MatrixParam("name")
                    String name) {

      return Response
                  .status(200)
                  .entity("Id: " + id + ", Name: " + name)
                  .build();
}
```

In this example, we have used the `@MatrixParameter` annotation to map the `id` and `name` parameters with the request `id` and `name` parameters respectively.

The bean parameter

To set the bean parameters, we can use any of the `*Param` methods as follows:

```
WebTarget target = client
.target("http://localhost:8080/Chapter2/services/beanResource/get/101;
name=John;age=25?address=USA");

String responseData = target.request().get(String.class);
```

Or

```
WebTarget target = client.target("http://localhost:8080/Chapter2
services/beanResource/get");

String responseData =
  target
            .path("{id}")
            .resolveTemplate("id", "1001")
            .matrixParam("name", "John")
            .matrixParam("age", 25)
            .queryParam("address", "USA")
            .request()
            .get(String.class);
```

At the time of request invocation, the builder forms the URI as follows:

```
http://localhost:8080/Chapter2/services/beanResource/get/101;name=Joh
n;age=25?address=USA
```

On the server side, using an `@BeanParam` annotation provided by the JAX-RS API, different `*Parameters` are mapped to the `*Parameters` method respectively as follows:

```
@GET
@Path("/get/{id}")
public String get(@BeanParam UserBean user) {
    return "User Bean: " + user.toString();
}
```

The `UserBean` class can be used as follows:

```
public class UserBean {
    @PathParam("id")
    private String id;

    @MatrixParam("name")
    private String name;
```

```
        @MatrixParam("age")
        private String age;

        @DefaultValue("No address provided")
        @QueryParam("address")
        private String address;

        @HeaderParam("user-agent")
        private String userAgent;

        public String toString(){
           return
                  "Id: " + id +
                  ", Name: " + name +
                  ", Age: " + age +
                  ", Address: " + address +
                  ", User Agent: " + userAgent + "\n" ;
        }
    }
```

In this example, we have used the `@BeanParameter` annotation to map the `id`, `name`, `age`, `address` (optional), and `user Agent` parameters with request `id`, `name`, `age`, `address`, and `user Agent` parameters respectively.

The @Produces annotation

At times, we have multiple response MIME types implemented in resource classes. If we need a specific response MIME type, we need to provide the MIME type in the `request(MediaType)` method explicitly:

```
WebTarget target = client
  .target("http://localhost:8080/Chapter2/services/getResource/
getUserList");
String responseData = target
  .request(MediaType.APPLICATION_XML).get(String.class);
```

In this example, we have explicitly mentioned that the response MIME type should be `APPLICATION_XML`.

On the server side, using the `@Produces` annotation provided by the JAX-RS API, maps the request MIME type:

```
@GET
@Path("/getUserList")
@Produces({ "application/xml" })
public User[] getList() {
    User[] list = new User[3];
    list[0] = new User("John");
```

```
        list[1] = new User("William);
        list[2] = new User("Suzzane");

        return list;
    }
```

The `User` class can be used as follows:

```
    @XmlRootElement
    public class User {
        private String name;

        public User() {
        }

        public User(String name) {
            this.name = name;
        }

        public String getName() {
            return name;
        }

        public void setName(String name) {
            this.name = name;
        }

        @Override
        public String toString() {
            return name;
        }
    }
```

We don't need to convert the `List<User>` instance to an XML format. JAX-RS does this on its own.

The @Consumes annotation

At times, we have multiple accept MIME types that are implemented in resource classes. If we need a specific accept MIME type to process the request, we need to provide the MIME type in the `accept(MediaType)` object explicitly.

```
WebTarget target = client
.target("http://localhost:8080/Chapter2/services/postResource/
usingFormParamWithConsume");

MultivaluedMap<String, String> postForm = new
MultivaluedHashMap<String, String>();
```

```
postForm.add("name", "John");

String responseData = target
                .request()

.accept(MediaType.APPLICATION_FORM_URLENCODED_TYPE)
                .post(Entity.form(postForm),String.class) ;
```

In this example, we have explicitly mentioned that the accept MIME type should be `APPLICATION_FORM_URLENCODED_TYPE`.

On the server side, use the `@Consumes` annotation provided by the JAX-RS API to map the accept MIME type.

```
@POST
@Path("/usingFormParamWithConsume")
@Consumes(MediaType.APPLICATION_FORM_URLENCODED)
public String greet(@FormParam("name") String name) {
    return "Hello, " + name;
}
```

Use of Invocation.Builder

For invoking an HTTP request, we require an instance of Invocation Builder. An Invocation Builder instance is created using the web target's request method. Invocation Builder is basically used for wrapping up response media type, headers, properties, authentication token, cookies, and so on. These can be used for data manipulation or authentication at the server side. Let's look at the following example:

```
WebTarget target = client.target("http://localhost:8080/Chapter2/
services/getResource");

Invocation.Builder builder = target.request("text/plain");

Invocation invocation = builder.buildGet();

String responseData = invocation.invoke(String.class);
```

Here, we first created an instance of `WebTarget` for the URI from the client instance. We set the accept type in the request and set the instance to `Invocation.Builder`. We then wrapped the Builder instance to Invocation; that is, our request is ready with the headers/properties, data, and so on, and ready to call the web service. Using the `invoke(T)` object, we call the web service. In this, we are expecting `String.class` to be the response. Else, we can also have a response instance from the web service using `invoke()` as shown in the following example:

```
Response response = invocation.invoke();

String responseData = response.readEntity(String.class);
```

Adding support for new representations

JAX-RS provides us the facility to add our custom entity provider for request/response message bodies. By using the custom entity provider, we can serialize or deserialize any message bodies with any media type. Using `MessageBodyReader<T>` for request and `MessageBodyWriter<T>` for response, we can implement these representations.

Before consuming a web service, we need to register the entity providers with any of the following methods: ClientBuilder or Client or WebTarget or ClientConfig.

Client transport connectors

Transport connectors are basically used to traverse the data to and from over the network. By default, HTTPURLConnection is used at the transport layer. On the base of Jersey-specific connector **Service Provider Interface (SPI)**, the HttpUrlConnector is wrapped to support the Jersey transport layer. We can create our own connector for transport layers. Alternatively, we can use ApacheConnector or GrizzlyConnector that are available in the market.

Securing a client

To secure communication between request-response instances in our application, we can implement **Secure Sockets Layer (SSL)**. Jersey client provides us a way to use SSL by using SSLContext. This will be used during communication to the server endpoint from the Jersey client instance. Here's an example that shows how to implement SSL:

```
SSLContext sslContext = SSLContext.getInstance("SSL");

Client client = ClientBuilder.newBuilder().sslContext(sslContext).
build();

Response response = client
.target("https://localhost:8080/Chapter2/services/getResource").
request().get();
```

In this example, we created an instance of SSLContext that is passed as a constructor argument in the ClientBuilder instance. The `SSLContext.getInstance(String)` provides us the specified secure socket protocol.

Summary

JAX-RS 2.0 Client API provides us a simple API for consuming web services. In this chapter, we covered Client API and how to use different HTTP methods and *Param annotations for consuming web services. We also covered the web service flow from the client request to server response. This API provides an easier way for a developer to utilize its simplified API. We can also create our own custom MIME type and its implementation using MessageBodyReader<T> for request and MessageBodyWriter<T>. Lastly, we checked how we can secure our application by implementing SSL. In the next chapter, we will see how we can use different media representations (JSON, XML, and Multipart) for data interchange between the client and server. These media representations are important, because they define how the web services data will look.

4
Common Media-Type Representations

In this chapter, we will learn how to use different representations of data. **Data representation** is the primary decision for any application. We need to decide appropriate representation on the basis of the client that will consume the web services. We will also go through the implementation of different representations on the server side, as well as on the client side.

JSON

JSON is a lightweight format used to traverse the network. It is easy to parse and generate a JSON format from POJOs and Java types. The following modules are supported by Jersey JSON:

- MOXy
- Java API for JSON Processing (JSON-P)
- Jackson
- Jettison

Let's look at each in turns.

MOXy

The **MOXy** component allows developers to bind POJOs to XML or JSON formats. It automatically formats data without any explicit configuration. This MOXy feature is automatically discovered when you add the jersey-media module in an application. MOXy combines with JAXB and manages to convert data to and fro. Let's check how we can use MOXy in our application:

```
public class App extends ResourceConfig {
    public App() {
        packages("com.chapter4").register
        (new JsonMoxyConfigurationContextResolver());
    }

    @Provider
    final static class JsonMoxyConfigurationContextResolver
    implements ContextResolver<MoxyJsonConfig> {

        @Override
        public MoxyJsonConfig getContext(Class<?> objectType) {
            final MoxyJsonConfig configuration = new MoxyJsonConfig();

            Map<String, String> namespacePrefixMapper =
            new HashMap<String, String>(1);
            namespacePrefixMapper.put(
              "http://www.w3.org/2001/XMLSchema-instance", "xsi");

            configuration.setNamespacePrefixMapper(namespacePrefixMap
              per);
            configuration.setNamespaceSeparator(':');

            return configuration;
        }
    }
}
```


In this example, we registered `JsonMoxyConfigurationContextResolver` that implements `MoxyJsonConfig`. In `JsonMoxyConfigurationContextResolver`, we set the property of `MoxyJsonConfig`. This enables us to use the `MOXy` feature. When MOXy is explicitly disabled, it is necessary to register `MOXyJsonProvider`. Let's look at how to register `MOXyJsonProvider` using the abstract `Application` class.

We can override the `getSingletons()` method of the `Application` class to register `MOXyJsonProvider`:

```
public class UsingApplication extends Application {
    @Override
    public Set<Class<?>> getClasses() {
        Set<Class<?>> s = new HashSet<Class<?>>();
        s.add(UserResource.class);
        return s;
    }

    @Override
    public Set<Object> getSingletons() {
        MOXyJsonProvider moxyJsonProvider =
          new MOXyJsonProvider();
        moxyJsonProvider.setWrapperAsArrayName(true);
        HashSet<Object> set = new HashSet<Object>(1);
        set.add(moxyJsonProvider);
        return set;
    }
}
```

In the `getSingletons()` method, we enabled the grouping of the element that should be used as the JSON array name using the `wrapperAsArrayName` property on `MOXyJsonProvider`.

Using ResourceConfig class

We registered `JsonMoxyConfigurationContextResolver` that implements `MoxyJsonConfig`:

```
public class UsingResourceConfig extends ResourceConfig {

    public UsingResourceConfig() {
        packages("com.chapter4").register
          (new JsonMoxyConfigurationContextResolver());
    }

    @Provider
    final static class JsonMoxyConfigurationContextResolver
    implements ContextResolver<MoxyJsonConfig> {

        @Override
        public MoxyJsonConfig getContext(Class<?> objectType) {
            final MoxyJsonConfig configuration = new MoxyJsonConfig();
```

```
            Map<String, String> namespacePrefixMapper =
              new HashMap<String, String>(1);
            namespacePrefixMapper.put(
              "http://www.w3.org/2001/XMLSchema-instance", "xsi");

            configuration.setNamespacePrefixMapper
              (namespacePrefixMapper);
            configuration.setNamespaceSeparator(':');

            return configuration;
        }
    }
}
```

In `JsonMoxyConfigurationContextResolver`, we set the property of `MoxyJsonConfig`. This enables us to use the MOXy feature. When MOXy is explicitly disabled, it is necessary to register `MOXyJsonProvider`.

> Note: To use MOXy as your JSON provider, you need to add the jersey-media-moxy module.

Java API for JSON Processing (JSON-P)

In JAX-RS 2.0, this feature can be automatically discovered. We don't need to explicitly register the JSON-P feature. It just needs to be added into our application. Let's see how to use JSON-P:

- On the server side:

  We will register `JsonProcessingFeature` into the server application and `JsonGenerator.PRETTY_PRINTING` property. This needs to be done when the application is loaded, so the application can make use of `JsonProcessingFeature` for marshaling and unmarshaling the data interchange on the server side:

```
public class UsingResourceConfig extends ResourceConfig {
    public UsingResourceConfig() {
        packages("com.chapter4.jsonp")
          .register(JsonProcessingFeature.class)
          .property(JsonGenerator.PRETTY_PRINTING, true);
    }
}
```

- On the client side:

  Here also, we need to register `JsonProcessingFeature` to enable the marshaling and unmarshaling of data interchange on the client side:

  ```
  Client client = ClientBuilder.newBuilder()
    .register(JsonProcessingFeature.class)
    .property(JsonGenerator.PRETTY_PRINTING, true)
    .build();
  ```

  Here, `JsonProcessingFeature` is registered and the `JsonGenerator.PRETTY_PRINTING` property is set to true. This should be registered when `JsonProcessingFeature` is explicitly disabled.

> Note that in order to use JSON-P as your JSON provider, you need to add the jersey-media-json-processing module.

Jackson

Jackson JSON processor is a powerful API that serves the function of binding data between POJO and JSON. For creating a custom implementation of serialization/deserialization, we need to create our own custom `ObjectMapper` instance, and this instance needs to be registered at the client and server sides. Also, we need to register `JacksonFeature` on both sides. Let's see how we can implement it:

- On the server side:

  ```
  public class UsingResourceConfig extends ResourceConfig {
      public UsingResourceConfig() {
          packages("com.chapter4.jackson")
             .register(MyObjectMapperProvider.class)
      // if needed
             .register(JacksonFeature.class);
      }
  }
  ```

  We can see that `JacksonFeature` and `MyObjectMapperProvider` are registered at the initial application loading, so as to use `JacksonFeature`.

- On the client side:

  ```
  Client client = ClientBuilder.newBuilder()
    .register(MyObjectMapperProvider.class) // if needed
    .register(JacksonFeature.class)
    .build();
  ```

  Here also, we need to register `JacksonFeature` and `MyObjectMapperProvider` to provide support for the marshaling and unmarshaling of data interchange on the client side.

- On both the sides:

```
@Provider
public class MyObjectMapperProvider implements
ContextResolver<ObjectMapper> {

    /**
    Default Object Mapper will be used for other POJOs
    */
    final ObjectMapper defaultObjectMapper;

    /**
    user Object Mapper will be used for User POJO ONLY.
    */
    final ObjectMapper userObjectMapper;

    /**
    MyObjectMapperProvider() constructor initializes the
    defaultObjectMapper and userObjectMapper.
    */
    public MyObjectMapperProvider() {
        defaultObjectMapper = createDefaultMapper();
        userObjectMapper = createUserObjectMapper();
    }

/**
```

This method provides the specific `ObjectMapper` instance. Either it can be `UserObjectMapper` for the user POJO or `DefaultObjectMapper` for the other POJOs.

```
*/
    @Override
    public ObjectMapper getContext(Class<?> type) {
        if (type == User.class) {
        return userObjectMapper;
        } else {
        return defaultObjectMapper;
        }
    }

/**
```

This method returns the `UserObjectMapper` instance by configuring the properties to use specific serialization and deserialization mechanism. This helps to wrap the data in request/response.

```
*/
    private static ObjectMapper createUserObjectMapper() {
        Pair combinedIntrospector =
       createJaxbJacksonAnnotationIntrospector();
        ObjectMapper result = new ObjectMapper();
        result.configure(SerializationConfig.Feature.
          WRAP_ROOT_VALUE, true);
        result.configure(DeserializationConfig.
          Feature.UNWRAP_ROOT_VALUE, true);
        result.setDeserializationConfig(
            result.getDeserializationConfig()
              .withAnnotationIntrospector
              (combinedIntrospector));
            result.setSerializationConfig(
            result.getSerializationConfig()
            .withAnnotationIntrospector(combinedIntrospector));

        return result;
    }

/**
```

This method provides the `DefaultObjectMapper` instance that can be used for any POJO other than a specific defined `ObjectMapper` POJO:

```
*/
    private static ObjectMapper createDefaultMapper() {
        ObjectMapper result = new ObjectMapper();
        result.configure(Feature.INDENT_OUTPUT, true);

        return result;
    }

/**
```

This method provides the pair of the annotation introspectors that transforms JAXB annotation to a JSON mapping:

```
*/
    private static Pair createJaxbJacksonAnnotationIntrospector() {

        AnnotationIntrospector jaxbIntrospector =
          new JaxbAnnotationIntrospector();
```

```
            AnnotationIntrospector jacksonIntrospector =
              new JacksonAnnotationIntrospector();
            return new AnnotationIntrospector.Pair(
            jacksonIntrospector, jaxbIntrospector);
        }
    }
```

Here, we have created our own custom `ObjectMapper` implementation that handles the user POJO, as well as the other POJOs. You can find the difference in implementation in the `createDefaultMapper()` and `createUserObjectMapper()` methods.

> Note that in order to use Jackson as your JSON provider, you need to add the jersey-media-json-jackson module.

Jettison

Jettison is a JSON API that is used to parse and generate JSON formats. We need to register `JettisonFeature` and `ContextResolver<T>` for JAXB POJO at both ends. Let's look at how we can implement it:

- On the server side:

  ```
  public class UsingResourceConfig extends ResourceConfig {
      public UsingResourceConfig() {
          packages("com.chapter4.jettison")
            .register(CustomContextResolver.class)
            // if needed
            .register(JettisonFeature.class);
      }
  }
  ```

  We can see that `JettisonFeature` and `CustomContextResolver` are registered at the initial application loading to enable the use of `JettisonFeature`.

- On the client side:

  ```
  Client client = ClientBuilder.newBuilder()
    .register(CustomContextResolver.class)  // if needed
    .register(JettisonFeature.class)
    .build();
  ```

  As on the server side, we need to register `JettisonFeature` and `CustomContextResolver` when the client instance is being created.

- On both the sides:

```
@Provider
public class CustomContextResolver implements
ContextResolver<JAXBContext> {

    private final JAXBContext context;
    private final Set<Class<?>> types;
    private final Class<?>[] cTypes = {User.class};

    public CustomContextResolver() throws Exception {
        this.types =
          new HashSet<Class<?>>(Arrays.asList(cTypes));
        this.context = new JettisonJaxbContext(
        JettisonConfig.DEFAULT, cTypes);
    }

    @Override
    public JAXBContext getContext(Class<?> objectType) {
        return (types.contains(objectType)) ?
          context : null;
    }
}
```

> In the preceding example, `ContextResolver<T>` is optional. If any special processing has to be done, we can use `ContextResolver<T>`. We defined user POJO to be marshaled and unmarshaled using the Jettison feature. To use Jettison as your JSON provider, you need to add the jersey-media-json-jettison module.

XML

XML is a standard way to process data in the client/server architecture. Jersey provides different ways to use XML for data traversing over the client/server.

Low-level XML support

Low-level XML support consists of:

- StreamSource
- SAXSource
- DOMSource
- Document

Let's look at the following example:

- Server side:

```
@Path("/userResource")
public class UserResource {

    @POST
    @Path("usingStreamSource")
    public StreamSource getStreamSource(StreamSource streamSource)
    {
        return streamSource;
    }

    @POST
    @Path("usingSAXSource")
    public SAXSource getSAXSource(SAXSource saxSource) {
        return saxSource;
    }

    @POST
    @Path("usingDOMSource")
    public DOMSource getDOMSource(DOMSource domSource) {
        return domSource;
    }

    @POST
    @Path("usingDocument")
    public Document getDocument(Document document) {
        return document;
    }
}
```

StreamSource, SAXSource, DOMSource, and Document are different types of XML formats. These low-level formats are used to read, parse, or generate XMLs using their simplified APIs.

- Client side:

```
WebTarget target =
client.target("http://localhost:8080/Chapter4_XML/services/
userResource/usingStreamSource");

User bean = target.request(MediaType.APPLICATION_XML).post(
Entity.entity(new User(1,"John"),
    MediaType.APPLICATION_XML),User.class) ;
```

This is the format used to read, parse, or generate XMLs using their simplified APIs on the client side. It follows the same way for SAXSource, DOMSource, and Document URI.

JAXB support

The JAXB annotation is simple to map POJO with the XML elements. We just have to assign `@XmlRootElement` to our POJO, and then JAXB handles the data by itself. Let's look at the following example:

- Server side:

```
@Path("jaxbResource")
@Produces("application/xml")
@Consumes("application/xml")
public class UserResource {

    @GET
    public User[] getUserArray() {
        List<User> userList = new ArrayList<User>();
        userList.add(new User(1, "John"));
        .........
        return userList.toArray(new User[userList.size()]);
    }
}
```

  This root-resource class produces and consumes XML MIME types only. The MIME type is defined at the class level, so by default all the resource methods and subresource methods will have the same MIME type.

- Client side:

```
.........
WebTarget target =
client.target("http://localhost:8080/Chapter4_XML/services/
jaxbResource");

GenericType<User[]> userListGenericType = new
GenericType<User[]>() {};
User[] responseData =
target.request
(MediaType.APPLICATION_XML).get(userListGenericType);

for(User  user : responseData)
{
    System.out.println("Response Data: " + user);
}
```

Here, because we are getting `User[]` in response, we use `GenericType<T>` to obtain the response entity along with the XML media type. We can also create custom `GenericType<T>` by subclassing it in order to use it as an entity in request and response. `GenericType<T>` is basically used for objects that have parameterized type.

- Both sides:

```
@XmlRootElement
public class User {
    private int id;
    private String name;

    public User() {}

    public User(int id,String name) {
        this.id = id;
        this.name = name;
    }
    .........
}
```

Here, the `@XmlRootElement` JAXB annotation maps the user object to the XML elements. The name of the root XML element will be the class name.

POJOs

In this media type representation, beans are not assigned any annotations. We programmatically map the POJOs to the XML elements. This is shown in the following example:

- Server side:

```
@GET
@Path("withoutAnnotation")
public JAXBElement<UserWithoutAnnotation> getuser() {

    UserWithoutAnnotation user = new UserWithoutAnnotation
(1,"John");

    return new JAXBElement<UserWithoutAnnotation>
    (new QName("user"), UserWithoutAnnotation.class, user);
}
```

Here, we responded to the `JAXBElement` instance that contains the `UserWithoutAnnotation` POJO. `QName` is the qualified name, which is used for assigning the root element name.

- Client side:

```
.........
WebTarget target = client.target("http://localhost:8080/Chapter4_
XML/services/jaxbResource/withoutAnnotation");

GenericType<JAXBElement<UserWithoutAnnotation>> userType =
new GenericType<JAXBElement<UserWithoutAnnotation>>() {};


UserWithoutAnnotation user = (UserWithoutAnnotation) target
.request(MediaType.APPLICATION_XML_TYPE)
.get(userType)
.getValue();
.........
```

Here, we obtain the `UserWithoutAnnotation` response POJO using the `getValue()` method. The `getValue()` method automatically maps the XML to the `UserWithoutAnnotation` POJO. Else, we can also obtain the XML format in response using:

```
target.request(MediaType.APPLICATION_XML_TYPE).get(String.class);
```

And then, we can access it using any XML parser.

Multipart

At times, we require multipart representation in request/response web services. We need to create custom `MessageBodyReader<T>` and `MessageBodyWriter<T>` implementation to support the multipart feature in our application. For this, we need to register `MultiPartFeature` on the client and server sides. Look at the following example:

- Server side:

```
public class UsingResourceConfig extends ResourceConfig {

    public UsingResourceConfig() {
        packages("com.chapter4.multipart")
        .register(MultiPartFeature.class);
    }
}
```

Here, we registered `MultiPartFeature` at the time of application loading. This feature needs to be registered to provide the marshalling and unmarshalling of data on the server side.

```
@POST
@Consumes(MediaType.MULTIPART_FORM_DATA)
public String post(
    @FormDataParam("part") String part,
    @FormDataParam("part") FormDataContentDisposition d)
    {
        return part + ":" + d.getFileName();
    }
```


In this `post()` method, it accepts `FormDataParam`, which contains the form value, and `FormDataContentDisposition`, which contains the metadata or header of the file.

- Client side:

```
Client client = ClientBuilder
.newBuilder()
.register(MultiPartFeature.class)
.build();
```

Here, we registered `MultiPartFeature` on the client side. This enables us to use multipart representation between the client/server data interchange.

```
    .....
WebTarget target = client.target("http://localhost:8080/Chapter4_
Multipart/services/
 multipartResource");

final FormDataMultiPart multipart = new FormDataMultiPart();

final FormDataBodyPart bodyPart = new  FormDataBodyPart
(FormDataContentDisposition.name("part").fileName("file").
build(),"CONTENT");

multipart.bodyPart(bodyPart);

String response = target.request().post(Entity.entity(multipart,
MediaType.MULTIPART_FORM_DATA_TYPE), String.class);
    .....
```

Here, we created the instance of `FormDataMultipart` that will contain the multipart request to be sent to the server. `FormDataBodyPart` will have the form data and files to be attached.

> Note that in order to use multipart features, you need to add the jersey-media-multipart module.

Summary

We've analyzed different media type representations that are useful for data interchange between the client and server sides. These media type representations should be chosen on the basis of requirement, which best fit the situation. We also need to keep in mind that the same web services can be accessed with different representations, that is, JSON and XML both can be consumed. Then, it becomes easier for us to create and manage the web service, because most media type representations are managed by Jersey itself. In the next chapter, we will see how to create and consume the **Server-Sent Events (SSE)**. SSE is a nice feature that has support from the client and server APIs.

5
Server-Sent Events (SSE)

In the previous chapters, we covered how to create and consume the RESTful web services using JAX-RS 2.0 and Jersey 2.0. In this chapter, we will learn how to create a connection between the client/server and maintain the connection at the server end. This is required to push data from the server to the client without any new request being initiated by the client. Basically, this type of mechanism is used for applications, such as chatting, stock market, or any real-time data-providing applications.

Getting started

Generally, the flow of web services is initiated by the client by sending a request for the resource to the server. This is the traditional way of consuming web services.

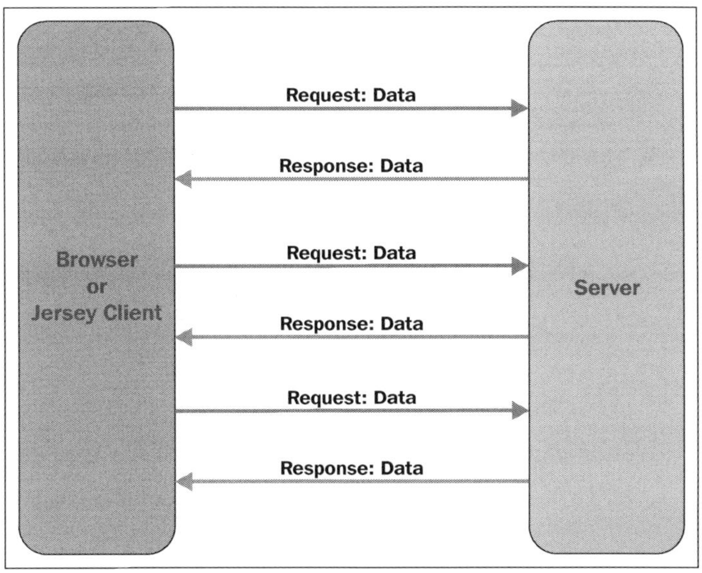

Traditional Flow

Here, the browser or Jersey client initiates the request for data from the server, and the server provides a response along with the data. Every time a client needs to initiate a request for the resource, the server may not have the capability to generate the data. This becomes difficult in an application where real-time data needs to be shown. Even though there is no new data over the server, the client needs to check for it every time.

Nowadays, there is a requirement that the server needs to send some data without the client's request. For this to happen the client and server need to be connected, and the server can push the data to the client. This is why it is termed as Server-Sent Events. In these events, the connections created initially between the client and server are not released after the request. The server maintains the connection and pushes the data to the respective client when required.

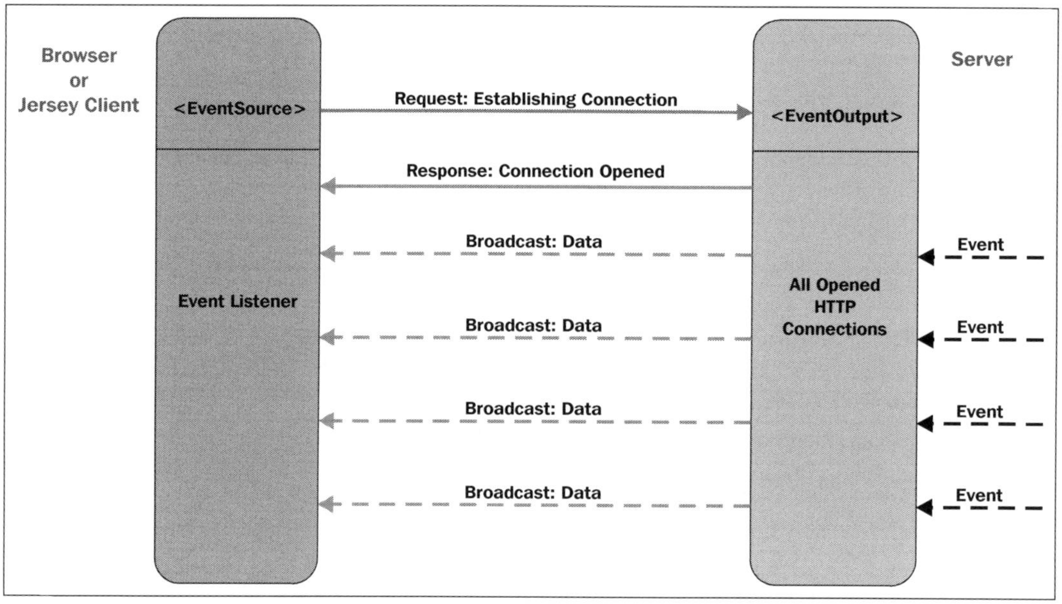

Server-Sent Event Flow

In the Server-Sent Event Flow diagram initially, when a browser or a Jersey client initiates a request to establish a connection with the server using `EventSource`, the server is always in a listening mode for the new connection to be established. When a new connection from any `EventSource` is received, the server opens a new connection and maintains it in a queue. Maintaining a connection depends upon the implementation of business logic. SSE create a single unidirectional connection. So, only a single connection is established between the client and server.

After the connection is successfully established, the client is in the listening mode for new events from the server. Whenever any new event occurs on the server side, it will broadcast the event, along with the data to a specific open HTTP connection. In modern browsers that support HTML5, the `onmessage` method of `EventSource` is responsible for handling new events received from the server; whereas, in the case of Jersey clients, we have the `onEvent` method of `EventSource`, which handles new events from the server.

> Note: Server-Sent Event creates a single unidirectional connection.

Implementing Server-Sent Events (SSE)

To use SSE, we need to register `SseFeature` on both the client and server sides. By doing so, the client/server gets connected to `SseFeature` to be used while traversing data over the network.

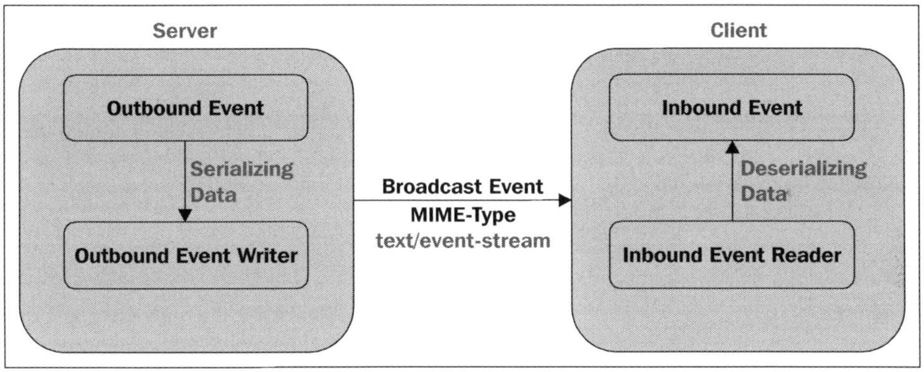

SSE: Internal Working

In the SSE: Internal Working diagram, we assume that the client/server is connected. When any new event is generated, the server initiates an `OutboundEvent` instance that will be responsible to have chunked output, which in turn will have a serialized data format. `OutboundEventWriter` is responsible to serialize the data on the server side. We need to specify the media type of the data in `OutboundEvent`. There are no restrictions of providing specific media types only.

However, on the client side, `InboundEvent` is responsible for handling the incoming data from the server. Here, `InboundEvent` receives the chunked input that contains serialized data format. Using `InbounEventReader`, data is deserialized.

Using `SSEBroadCaster`, we are able to broadcast events to multiple clients that are connected to the server. Let's look at the example, which shows how to create SSE web services and broadcast the events:

```
@ApplicationPath("services")
public class SSEApplication extends ResourceConfig {
    publicSSEApplication() {
        super(SSEResource.class, SseFeature.class);
    }
}
```

Here, we registered the `SseFeature` module and the `SSEResource` root-resource class to the server.

```
private static final SseBroadcaster BROADCASTER = new
SseBroadcaster();
......
@GET
@Path("sseEvents")
@Produces(SseFeature.SERVER_SENT_EVENTS)
public EventOutput getConnection() {

    final EventOutput eventOutput = new EventOutput();

    BROADCASTER.add(eventOutput);

    return eventOutput;
}
......
```

In the `SSEResource` root class, we need to create a resource method that will allow clients to establish the connection and persist accordingly. Here, we are maintaining the connection into the `BROADCASTER` instance in the `SseBroadcaster` class. `EventOutput` manages specific client connections. `SseBroadcaster` is simply responsible for accommodating a group of `EventOutput`; that is, the client's connection.

```
......
@POST
@Consumes(MediaType.APPLICATION_FORM_URLENCODED)
public void post(@FormParam("name") String name) {
    BROADCASTER
        .broadcast(new OutboundEvent.Builder()
        .data(String.class, name)
        .build());
}
......
```

When any post method is consumed, we create a new event and broadcast it to the client available in the `BROADCASTER` instance. The `OutboundEvent` instance will contain the data (`MediaType`, `Object`) method that is initialized with a specific media type and actual data. We can provide any media type to send data. By using the `build()` method, data is being serialized with the `OutBoundEventWriter` class internally. When the broadcast `(OutboundEvent)` is called, internally `SseBroadcaster` pushes data on all registered `EventOutputs`; that is, on clients connected to `SseBroadcaster`.

At times, there's a scenario where the client/server has been connected and after sometime, the client gets disconnected. So, in this case, `SseBroadcaster` automatically handles the client connection; that is, it determines whether the connection needs to be maintained. When any client connection is closed, the broadcaster detects `EventOutput` and frees the connection and resources obtained by that `EventOutput` connection.

> Note: To use SSE we need to include the jersey-media-sse module.

Consuming the SSE events

Jersey client has two models that can consume SSE:

- The pull model (Using `EventInput`)
- The push model (Using `EventSource`)

The pull model (Using EventInput)

The pull model allows us to read and consume events when they arrive. By using `EventInput`, we can access the data. Let's look at the example:

```
......
Client client = ClientBuilder
                    .newBuilder()
                    .register(SseFeature.class)
                    .build();

WebTarget target = client
                    .target("http://localhost:8080/
Chapter5_Server_Sent_Event/services/sseResource/sseEvents");

EventInputeventInput = target.request().get(EventInput.class);
```

```
while (!eventInput.isClosed()) {
    final InboundEvent inboundEvent = eventInput.read();
    if (inboundEvent == null) {
        break; // connection has been closed
    }
    try {
        System.out.println(inboundEvent.getData(String.class));
    } catch (IOException exception) {
        exception.printStackTrace();
    }
}
......
```

First, we created an instance of a client that has registered `SseFeature`. We then mapped `WebTarget` to the SSE resource method, which can provide a connection between the client and server. Next, we invoked the `gethttp` method, requesting the media type to respond as `EventInput`. Here, the server returns the `EventInput` type, which means connection is being established between the client and server. Once the connection stream is closed from the server end, the `EventInput` type will also release the connection from the client end. `EventInput` is an extension of `ChunkedInput<InboundEvent>` that allows us to read the event data using the inbound event's `getData(MediaType)` method.

The push model (using EventSource)

The push model is basically used for reading and processing asynchronous events using `EventSource`. Let's look at the following example:

```
......
Client client = ClientBuilder
                    .newBuilder()
                    .register(SseFeature.class)
                    .build();

WebTarget target = client
                    .target("http://localhost:8080/
Chapter5_Server_Sent_Event/services/sseResource/sseEvents");

final EventSource eventSource = new EventSource(target) {

    @Override
    public void onEvent(InboundEvent inboundEvent) {
        try {
```

```
                System.out.println("Data Received: " + inboundEvent.
                  getData(String.class));
            } catch (Exception e) {
                e.printStackTrace();
            }
        }
    };
    ......
```

In this example, we first created instance of client that have registered `SseFeature`. Then, we pointed our SSE resource URI to `WebTarget`. Using the `EventSource` constructor, we created the instance of `EventSource` that has an established connection with the server. So, we can process the SSE using the `onEvent(InboundEvent)` method and consume it using the `getData(MediaType)` method.

Summary

In this chapter, we learned the difference between the traditional web service flow and SSE web service flow. We also covered how to create the SSE web services and implement the Jersey client in order to consume the SSE using different programmatic models; that is, using `EventInput` and `EventSource`. In the next chapter, we will generate the **Web Application Description Language (WADL)** that defines the RESTful web application using XML.

6
WADL

In the previous chapters, we described and analyzed the implementation of the server and the client. In this chapter, we will describe the **Web Application Description Language (WADL)**, which is a skeleton of the deployed RESTful web service.

Getting started

WADL is an XML description for the deployed RESTful web service. It is supported using the Jersey implementation, and is similar to SOAP's **Web Services Description Language (WSDL)**.

Like WSDL that shows the structure, functionality, and parameters, and accepts different HTTP methods of the SOAP web services, WADL also provides the same features. The difference between the two is that WADL is used for RESTful-based web services, and WSDL is used for SOAP-based web services.

Let's see how WADL looks for our resource class:

```
@Path("/getResource")
public class GetResource {
    @GET
    public String get() {
        return "Hello World!!!";
    }

    @GET
    @Path("{name}")
    public Response greetUser(@PathParam("name") String name){
        returnResponse.status(200).entity("Hello, " +
        name).build();
    }
}
```

Here, we have two `@GET` resource methods under the `getResource` path. Once the application is deployed on the server, open the URI in a browser:

```
http://localhost:8080/Chapter6/services/application.wadl
```

Jersey automatically generates WADL from the resource classes. It will have a get method with the `/application.wadl` resource. This will give the following result:


```
<?xml version="1.0" encoding="UTF-8" standalone="yes"?>
<application xmlns="http://wadl.dev.java.net/2009/02">
    <doc xmlns:jersey="http://jersey.java.net/"
jersey:generatedBy="Jersey: 2.0 2013-05-03 14:50:15" />
    <grammars />
    <resources base="http://localhost:8080/Chapter6/services/">
        <resource path="/getResource">
            <method id="get" name="GET">
                <response />
            </method>
            <method id="apply" name="OPTIONS">
                <request>
                    <representation mediaType="*/*" />
                </request>
                <response>
                    <representation mediaType="application/vnd.sun.
                      wadl+xml" />
                </response>
            </method>
            <method id="apply" name="OPTIONS">
                <request>
                    <representation mediaType="*/*" />
                </request>
                <response>
                    <representation mediaType="text/plain" />
                </response>
            </method>
            <method id="apply" name="OPTIONS">
                <request>
                    <representation mediaType="*/*" />
                </request>
                <response>
                    <representation mediaType="*/*" />
```

```
            </response>
        </method>
        <resource path="{name}">
        <paramxmlns:xs="http://www.w3.org/2001/XMLSchema" name="name"
              style="template" type="xs:string"/>
            <method id="greetUser" name="GET">
                <response />
            </method>
            <method id="apply" name="OPTIONS">
                <request>
                    <representation mediaType="*/*" />
                </request>
                <response>
                    <representation mediaType="application/vnd.sun.
                      wadl+xml" />
                </response>
            </method>
            <method id="apply" name="OPTIONS">
                <request>
                    <representation mediaType="*/*" />
                </request>
                <response>
                    <representation mediaType="text/plain" />
                </response>
            </method>
            <method id="apply" name="OPTIONS">
                <request>
                    <representation mediaType="*/*" />
                </request>
                <response>
                    <representation mediaType="*/*" />
                </response>
            </method>
        </resource>
    </resource>
    <resource path="application.wadl">
        <method id="getWadl" name="GET">
            <response>
                <representation mediaType="application/vnd.sun.
                  wadl+xml" />
```

```
            <representation mediaType="application/xml" />
        </response>
    </method>
    <method id="apply" name="OPTIONS">
        <request>
            <representation mediaType="*/*" />
        </request>
        <response>
            <representation mediaType="text/plain" />
        </response>
    </method>
    <method id="apply" name="OPTIONS">
        <request>
            <representation mediaType="*/*" />
        </request>
        <response>
            <representation mediaType="*/*" />
        </response>
    </method>
    <resource path="{path}">
    <paramxmlns:xs="http://www.w3.org/2001/XMLSchema" name="path"
          style="template" type="xs:string"/>
        <method id="geExternalGrammar" name="GET">
            <response>
                <representation mediaType="application/xml" />
            </response>
        </method>
        <method id="apply" name="OPTIONS">
            <request>
                <representation mediaType="*/*" />
            </request>
            <response>
                <representation mediaType="text/plain" />
            </response>
        </method>
        <method id="apply" name="OPTIONS">
            <request>
                <representation mediaType="*/*" />
            </request>
            <response>
```

```
                    <representation mediaType="*/*" />
                </response>
            </method>
        </resource>
    </resource>
  </resources>
</application>
```

This is the WADL specification for the web service. In this WADL specification, we can see the first resource node as:

```
<resources base="http://localhost:8080/Chapter6/services/">
```

Here, `base` defines the prefix URI of the application through which web services are accessible. Under this resource node, there is another resource node, which is:

```
<resource path="/getResource">
```

This one defines the root class path. Using the `/getResource` path, we can access the resource method and subresource methods, such as `get()` and `greet()`. For each resource path, methods or subresource paths will be defined. Along with these methods or subresource paths, Jersey will create the `OPTIONS` method automatically. The method or subresource path will have the request and response parameter that defines the input parameters the web service takes, and the output parameter or entity or representation the web service returns back. These parameters are useful for the developers who are going to consume the web services during the implementation of the client side. As for the `PathParam` annotation, input parameters are defined under the resource path node as:

```
<resource path="{name}">
    <param name="name" style="template" type="xs:string"/>
.........
</resource>
```

To view WADL specifications for a specific root-resource class, we can use:

- Method: `OPTIONS`
- Accept type: `application/vnd.sun.wadl+xml`
- URI: `http://localhost:8080/Chapter6/services/getResource/John`

This will return a WADL specification as follows:

```
- <application>
    <doc jersey:generatedBy="Jersey: 2.0 2013-05-03 14:50:15"/>
    <grammars/>
  - <resources base="http://localhost:8080/Chapter6/services/">
    - <resource path="getResource/John">
      - <method id="greetUser" name="GET">
          <response/>
        </method>
      - <method id="apply" name="OPTIONS">
        - <request>
            <representation mediaType="*/*"/>
          </request>
        - <response>
            <representation mediaType="application/vnd.sun.wadl+xml"/>
          </response>
        </method>
      - <method id="apply" name="OPTIONS">
        - <request>
            <representation mediaType="*/*"/>
          </request>
        - <response>
            <representation mediaType="text/plain"/>
          </response>
        </method>
      - <method id="apply" name="OPTIONS">
        - <request>
            <representation mediaType="*/*"/>
          </request>
        - <response>
            <representation mediaType="*/*"/>
          </response>
        </method>
      </resource>
    </resources>
  </application>
```

This WADL specification only defines the XML description of the `greet()` method as we defined in the URI, to get only a specific path of WADL using the `OPTIONS` method.

Configuration

Jersey provides us with the facility to enable/disable the WADL creation. By default, WADL will be generated by Jersey. We explicitly have to define or disable the WADL creation. We can set the property in `web.xml` once the parameters are initialized, as follows:

```
<param-name>jersey.config.server.wadl.disableWadl</param-name>
<param-value>true</param-value>
```

If we use the deployment process using an application, then we need to use:

```
property(ServerProperties.WADL_FEATURE_DISABLE, true);
```

This will disable the WADL feature.

Summary

In this chapter, we documented how to generate the WADL specification of the web service. We also covered how the developer can find this WADL specification to consume or implement the web service for his/her reference. This WADL specification inform the developer about the input and output parameters that the web service takes in and out.

So far, we have covered all the major aspects of the JAX-RS 2.0 and Jersey 2.0, along with the theory and necessary coding part. Now, we are ready to tweak the API and create some complex applications.

Index

Symbols

A

B

C

D

L

M

P

Q

R

S

T

U

V

W

X

Thank you for buying
Developing RESTful Web Services with Jersey 2.0

About Packt Publishing

Packt, pronounced 'packed', published its first book "*Mastering phpMyAdmin for Effective MySQL Management*" in April 2004 and subsequently continued to specialize in publishing highly focused books on specific technologies and solutions.

Our books and publications share the experiences of your fellow IT professionals in adapting and customizing today's systems, applications, and frameworks. Our solution based books give you the knowledge and power to customize the software and technologies you're using to get the job done. Packt books are more specific and less general than the IT books you have seen in the past. Our unique business model allows us to bring you more focused information, giving you more of what you need to know, and less of what you don't.

Packt is a modern, yet unique publishing company, which focuses on producing quality, cutting-edge books for communities of developers, administrators, and newbies alike. For more information, please visit our website: `www.packtpub.com`.

About Packt Open Source

In 2010, Packt launched two new brands, Packt Open Source and Packt Enterprise, in order to continue its focus on specialization. This book is part of the Packt Open Source brand, home to books published on software built around Open Source licences, and offering information to anybody from advanced developers to budding web designers. The Open Source brand also runs Packt's Open Source Royalty Scheme, by which Packt gives a royalty to each Open Source project about whose software a book is sold.

Writing for Packt

We welcome all inquiries from people who are interested in authoring. Book proposals should be sent to author@packtpub.com. If your book idea is still at an early stage and you would like to discuss it first before writing a formal book proposal, contact us; one of our commissioning editors will get in touch with you.

We're not just looking for published authors; if you have strong technical skills but no writing experience, our experienced editors can help you develop a writing career, or simply get some additional reward for your expertise.

[PACKT] open source
community experience distilled
PUBLISHING

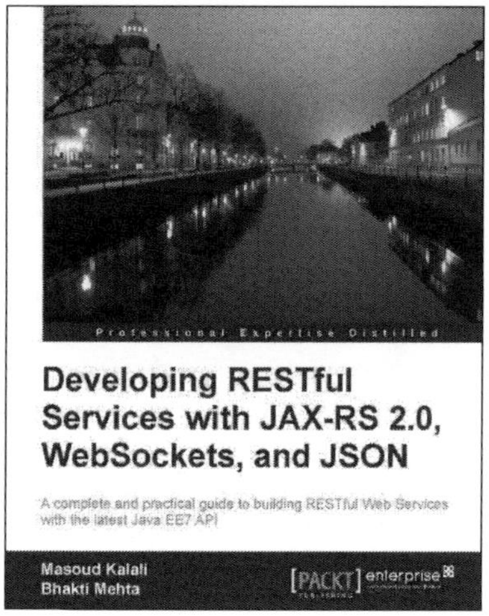

Developing RESTful Services with JAX-RS 2.0, WebSockets, and JSON

ISBN: 978-1-78217-812-5 Paperback: 128 pages

A complete and practical guide to building RESTful Web Services with the latest Java EE7 API

1. Learning about different client/server communication models including but not limited to client polling, Server-Sent Events and WebSockets

2. Efficiently use WebSockets, Server-Sent Events, and JSON in Java EE applications

3. Learn about JAX-RS 2.0 new features and enhancements

RESTful PHP Web Services

ISBN: 978-1-84719-552-4 Paperback: 220 pages

Learn the basic architectural concepts and steps through examples of consuming and creating RESTful web services in PHP

1. Get familiar with REST principles

2. Learn how to design and implement PHP web services with REST

3. Real-world examples, with services and client PHP code snippets

4. Introduces tools and frameworks that can be used when developing RESTful PHP applications

Please check **www.PacktPub.com** for information on our titles

5463636R00059

Printed in Germany
by Amazon Distribution
GmbH, Leipzig